Offray

TREASURES

FOR *Baby*

TREASURES
FOR *Baby*

EXQUISITE NURSERY DECORATIONS
AND HANDMADE RIBBON KEEPSAKES

Ellie Joos
Photography by George Ross

FRIEDMAN/FAIRFAX
PUBLISHERS

A FRIEDMAN/FAIRFAX BOOK

Please visit our website: www.metrobooks.com

© 2001 by Michael Friedman Publishing Group, Inc.

Library of Congress Cataloging-in-Publication data

Joos, Ellie.
    Offray treasures for baby : exquisite nursery decorations and handmade ribbon
  keepsakes / Ellie Joos ; photography by George Ross.
       p. cm.
    Includes bibliographical references and index.
    ISBN 1-56799-941-7 (alk. paper)
     1. Ribbon work. 2. Ribbon flowers. 3. Infants' supplies. I. Title.

    TT850.5 .J67 2001
    746'.0476—dc21
00-048467

Editor: Susan Lauzau
Art Director: Jeff Batzli
Designer: Orit Mardkha-Tenzer
Photography Director: Chris Bain
Production Manager: Richela Fabian Morgan
Illustrations: Steven Arcella
Photo Stylist: Karin Strom

Color separations by Spectrum Pte Ltd
Printed in Hong Kong by Midas Printing Limited

1 3 5 7 9 10 8 6 4 2

Distributed by Sterling Publishing Company, Inc.
387 Park Avenue South
New York, NY 10016
Distributed in Canada by Sterling Publishing
Canadian Manda Group
One Atlantic Avenue, Suite 105
Toronto, Ontario, Canada M6K 3E7
Distributed in Australia by
Capricorn Link (Australia) Pty Ltd.
P.O. Box 6651
Baulkham Hills, Business Centre, NSW 2153, Australia

Acknowledgments

IT IS HARD FOR ME TO BELIEVE that this is the third book I have now authored—the experience has been such a pleasure because of the talented individuals whose contributions have made this possible. First, a big thank you to my friends at Friedman/Fairfax, especially Chris Bain, from whom I have learned so much about photography lighting and composition. The results of his trained eye are evident in this book. Also, thank you to my editor Susan Lauzau for her patience and expertise.

Our team of experts included talented photographer George Ross and his assistant, Mary Ellen Stadtlander. Not only do they take great pictures, they are so much fun to work with! Team member Karin Strom, my dear friend and brilliant "vignette" designer, artfully accessorized and arranged each project for photography. Thank you so much to Susan and Bill Long and their delightful sons, Conner and Wyatt, who allowed us to rearrange both their rooms and their lives for several days.

Thank you also to the talented designers who collaborated with me to produce many of the projects using beautiful Offray ribbons—to my daughter-in-law, Nadia Fobert, and my friends Marinda Stewart, Nancy Keller, Elaine Schmidt, Miriam Gourley, Janis Bullis, and Marci Metzler. Thanks also to Marinda Stewart for the loan of her lovely baby items and to my friend Ricki Arno of Rosie's Creations, who made the exquisite hand-decorated almonds and sugar cubes.

A big hug and kiss to the special babies in my life, my grandchildren, Annabel Hope, Zachary, Alexandria, and Brooke, and my nephew Kevin, who sat so patiently for his photo. Thank you to Bill and my family for their continued love and support.

And last, but certainly not least, a very big thank you to Claude V. Offray, Jr., and my friends and fellow employees at Offray for designing and manufacturing the world's most beautiful ribbons.

Contents

Introduction

I WROTE MY LAST BOOK, *Offray's Glorious Weddings*, shortly after my son and daughter-in-law were married. I had a great time incorporating ideas from their wedding into that book, including the Unity candle, which featured their wedding invitation, and the ribbon rose–covered headbands I had made for the bride and her attendants. Their wedding photograph was featured in a beautiful pearl and ribbon frame that now sits on my desk.

As I wrote this book, the happy couple welcomed their second child, Annabel Hope. Zachary, their first, has been a real joy, and my relationship with him and with Allie, my husband's granddaughter, has yielded valuable information that I've included here, such as the child safety tips in the sidebar "Play it Safe." It is truly amazing how many things little ones can get into! I've also included quotes and tidbits of history and folklore that convey the excitement and joy with which new babies have always been greeted.

What makes this book so special, however, are the beautiful ribbon projects that allow parents-to-be and their families and friends to create unique gifts for the new arrival. As friends plan baby showers and the parents decorate the nursery, this book will serve as the perfect resource for charming shower favors, keepsake albums, one-of-a-kind birth announcements, inspired nursery accessories, and much more. All of these lovely projects can be made with simple materials and ribbons readily available at fabric and craft stores.

The start of a new generation is the perfect time to honor generations past by using the mementos saved and passed along; perhaps your family cherishes a vintage christening gown or an antique silver baby spoon. Perhaps you will wish to take this opportunity to create an heirloom-to-be by sewing the exquisite gown and bonnet featured in this book. We started with a commercial pattern and added rows of beautiful ribbons. I especially like the handkerchief bonnet in the "Baby's Homecoming" chapter. It is a lovely and simple gift to make for the new arrival.

I was fortunate enough to have my father's cradle when my son was born, and it has now been used by my grandchildren. You'll see it on page 46 with its newly fitted dust ruffle, bumpers, and pillows made from Battenburg lace sheets and coordinating lace-edged handkerchiefs trimmed with an array of white ribbons.

A new baby is certainly a blessing, a fresh opportunity to view the wonder of the world through their eyes and to appreciate all the little things in life. We at the Offray Ribbon Company and Friedman/Fairfax Publishers are so happy to share this special time with you, and wish you and your new arrival all the happiness in the world!!

—*Ellie Joos*

Chapter One

A Shower of Blessings

FRIENDS AND FAMILY CELEBRATE the baby's impending arrival with a "shower" of presents. Today, it is common for the parents-to-be to know the sex of the baby and to register at their favorite baby store, making gift-giving easier. One of the most practical and appreciated items to give is disposable diapers. Why not have some fun with the idea and create our Ribbon Diaper Centerpiece? When my granddaughter, Annabel Hope, was born, my daughter-in-law received such a centerpiece as a gift, and we loved it so much that she created the one featured here using ribbon roses and garlands for the frosting. Not only is it a fun centerpiece, it is entirely useful!

Picture frames and photo albums are also popular gifts. Ribbons and premade ribbon flowers add a pretty touch to simple wood or Lucite frames. An especially nice gesture is to make a frame that the new grandma can use to display photographs of her pride and joy.

Decorating for the shower calls for beautiful ribbons. Think of using ribbons to enhance napkins, chair backs, favors, and gift baskets and boxes. I'm sure the photographs shown here will inspire you to create a delightful setting for the mother-to-be. While you're at it, why not amuse your guests with some party diversions? See the sidebar "Baby Shower Games" for a few ideas that are most entertaining.

A Gift Basket for Baby

Fill a pretty basket with rattles, booties, and other accessories, and adorn it with ribbons in lively baby prints. Finish the basket off with a fresh flower bouquet for Mom, and you have the perfect shower or welcome-home gift.

MATERIALS

3–6 yds (3–5.5m) of several baby print ribbons

Basket

Shredded paper to fill basket

Gifts and toys to place in basket

DIRECTIONS

1. Fill basket three quarters full with shredded paper.

2. Glue ribbon around top edge of basket and handle if desired.

3. Using General Bow Techniques on page 140, make bows from remaining ribbons and wire them to basket handle.

4. Tie bows to assorted items and arrange in basket.

Babies are always more trouble than you thought—and more wonderful.

—CHARLES OSGOOD

Ribbon Diaper Centerpiece

One of the most useful gifts for the mother-to-be is disguised as a centerpiece shaped like a cake and decorated with ribbons and premade ribbon flowers. Essential baby items serve as the "candles."

MATERIALS

3½ yds (3.5m) of ⅞-inch (2cm)-wide, single-face satin ribbon

2½ yds (2.5m) of violet-petal garland in two colors

28 inches (70cm) of ⅝-inch (1.5cm)-wide single-face satin ribbon

2½ yds (2.5m) of ⅜-inch (1cm)-wide feather-edge satin ribbon

2½ yds (2.5m) rosebud garland

1⅔ yds (1.6m) of rosebud garland in a coordinating color

2 packages of premade small ribbon rosebuds

4 packages of premade medium ribbon roses

Circle of foamcore, 18 inches (50cm) in diameter

68 disposable diapers

1 paper towel tube, cut to 7 inches (17.5cm)

Clear packing tape

Double-stick tape

1 small toy for cake topper

Assorted small baby items (washcloths, bibs, toys, spoons, and pacifiers)

Glue gun and glue

DIRECTIONS

1. Glue paper towel tube to center of foamcore.

2. Set fourteen diapers aside for the top tier of the cake.

3. Tightly wrap remaining diapers around the base of the tube, opening each and securing each end with a small piece of packing tape. Overlap the last five diapers to hide the colorful waistband. The bottom tier should be approximately 48 inches (1.2 m) in circumference.

4. Wrap the bottom tier with one long length of packing tape.

5. Use the remaining fourteen diapers to create the top tier of the cake, following the same process described in Step 3. The top tier should be approximately 26 inches (66cm) in circumference.

TO DECORATE

1. Using double-stick tape, affix the $7/8$-inch-wide satin ribbon to the bottom and top edges of the cake's lower tier and to the bottom edge of the top tier.

2. Affix the $5/8$-inch-wide ribbon to the top edge of the cake's top tier.

3. Cut the violet-petal garlands into one 60-inch (1.5m) length and one 30-inch (76cm) length, and attach the longer garland to the $7/8$-inch-wide ribbon on the bottom edge of the lower tier. Repeat with the 30-inch length on the bottom edge of the top tier.

4. Cut the $3/8$-inch-wide feather-edge satin ribbons into two equal lengths and affix them to the center of the wide ribbons on the top edge of each tier.

5. Affix the $1 2/3$ yards-length of rosebud garland to the top edge of the bottom tier, allowing the rosebuds to create a scalloped design.

6. Cut $2 1/2$ yds garland into one 60-inch (1.5m) length and one 30-inch (76cm) length. Affix the 60-inch length of the rosebud garland to the top edge of the bottom tier to center of feather edge satin ribbon. Affix the remaining garland to top edge of top tier.

7. Tuck small baby items into the diapers to create a "candle" effect and add topper to cake. Add bunches of premade ribbon flowers to further decorate the cake.

BABY SHOWER GAMES

GUESS MOM'S GIRTH
Pass around a spool of ribbon, and tell each guest to cut off a length that they believe represents the circumference of the future mom's belly. The guest whose ribbon is closest to the correct length wins a prize.

WHAT'S IN THE BASKET?
Fill a basket with a number of useful baby items, preferably all in one color. Pass the basket around and allow each guest ten seconds to look at the basket. The guest who can recall the most items wins a prize.

BABY ANIMALS
Set a time limit and ask the guests to write down the names of as many baby animals as they can, for example, puppy, colt, kitten, and so on. Whoever has listed the most names wins a prize.

BABY BAG GAME
Put various baby items in different numbered brown paper bags and tie the tops closed with a pretty ribbon. Pass the bags around for guests and let them guess what is inside by feeling the bag.

Babies are such a nice way to start people.
—DON HEROLD

Boutique Hangers and Socks ⤳⤳⤳

Purchased padded hangers and infant socks look like costly boutique items when trimmed with ribbons and premade ribbon flowers.

Pale Yellow Hanger

MATERIALS

1¼ yds (1.25m) of ⅝-inch (1.5cm)-wide wire-edge ribbon

Variety of premade ribbon flowers

Padded satin-covered hanger, sized for baby clothes

Small crocheted doily

DIRECTIONS

1. Remove any existing ribbon from the padded hanger.

2. Make a hole in the center of doily. Place doily over hook. Glue to secure.

3. Following General Bow Techniques on page 140, make a double bow from wire-edge ribbon, leaving 3-inch (7.5cm) tails.

4. Tie bow to hook. Trim ends.

5. Glue premade ribbon flower to center of bow.

Aqua Hanger

MATERIALS

1½ yds (1.5m) of 1½-inch
(4cm)-wide sheer stripe ribbon
in aqua

⅞ yd (80cm) each of ⅛-inch
(3mm) and ¼-inch (6mm)-wide
ribbon in coordinating colors

Premade ribbon flowers

Padded satin-covered hanger, sized
for baby clothes

DIRECTIONS

1. Remove existing ribbon from padded hanger.

2. Cut 1½-inch-wide ribbon into one 32-inch (81cm) length and one 22-inch (56cm) length. Following General Bow Techniques on page 140, make a small four-loop bow from 1½-inch-wide ribbon, leaving 4-inch (10cm) tails. Using ⅛-inch and ¼-inch-wide ribbon, make two more four-loop bows, slightly smaller than the first bow. Glue the two smaller bows to the center of the large bow.

3. Tie the bow to the base of the hanger's hook with remaining 1½-inch-wide ribbon, wrap ribbon down around the hanger and back up to the hook. Tie once at the base of the hook.

4. Fold the ends of the ribbon over the center of the bow and tie in a knot.

5. Trim the ends of the ribbons. Glue a premade ribbon flower to center of the bow.

Little Socks

MATERIALS

2 premade ribbon flowers

2/3 yd (61 cm) of 1/2-inch (1.5cm) to 7/8-inch (2cm)-wide flat lace, cut in half

Purchased infant socks

DIRECTIONS

1. Stitch one length of lace to the top edge of one sock using a zigzag stitch. Stretch sock edge as you sew for a softly gathered edge.

2. Fold the sock cuff down. Hand stitch one ribbon flower to cuff and sock.

3. Repeat for other sock, stitching flower to opposite side of sock.

Hand-Decorated Picture Frames

T here are never enough frames for photographs of the new arrival, and these handmade charmers are sure to delight new parents. They also make thoughtful thank-yous from the baby's parents to the new grandparents.

Flowers and Bows Ribbon Frame

MATERIALS

1⅞ yds (1.75m) of ⅝-inch (1.5cm)-wide grosgrain ribbon

⅔ yd (61 cm) of premade ribbon flower garland

Premade ribbon flowers in assorted colors

5 x 7-inch (13 x 17.5cm) plastic picture frame

DIRECTIONS

1. Cut and glue grosgrain ribbon to outer edges of frame, either mitering corners or turning ends to back of frame and gluing in place.

2. Cut and glue lengths of ribbon flower garland to grosgrain ribbon around edge of frame. Watch placement of flowers so they align on top and bottom edges as well as side edges of frame.

5. Cut remaining grosgrain ribbon in half. Following General Bow Techniques on page 140, form each length into a small four-loop bow. Gather at the center with hand stitches.

6. Glue bows to upper corners of frame. Glue ribbon flowers to the center of each bow.

Ribbon and Paper Frame

MATERIALS

1⅓ yds (1.3m) of ⅝-inch (1.5cm)-wide wire-edge sheer rainbow ribbon

1 yd (1m) of 1½-inch (4cm)-wide wire-edge sheer pink ribbon

⅔ yd (61 cm) of ⅞-inch (2cm)-wide sheer ribbon in pink check

⅔ yd (61cm) of ⅞-inch (2cm)-wide sheer ribbon in green check

2 each premade sheer ribbon roses in pink and white

Heavy watercolor paper in a 22 x 30-inch (56 x 76cm) sheet

Pink paint

Paintbrush

Spray adhesive

DIRECTIONS

1. Tear one piece of watercolor paper so it measures 6½ inches by 8½ inches (16.5 x 21.5cm), the second piece to 7 inches by 9 inches (17.5 x 23cm), and the third piece to 7½ inches by 9½ inches (19 x 24cm), in order to create three layers for the frame. To create uneven edges for the paper frame, tear the watercolor paper against a straight edge or ruler.

2. The frame opening can be made to fit a specific photo. The sample shown has a 3½-inch (9cm)-square opening, which is centered toward the lower edge of the frame. Note that the largest frame section has the exact size opening needed; the middle-size frame section has a 4-inch (10cm) square opening, and the front frame section has a 4½-inch (11.5cm) square opening. To tear the opening, mark the appropriate opening size on the back of each frame section. Cut a hole in the center and then cut toward each corner. Pull flaps back from center and tear along the marked lines.

3. Paint outer and inner edges of the 7-by-9-inch frame section. Make sure painted area is about half an inch wide so that no unpainted areas show when the frame sections are glued together.

4. Using spray adhesive, glue the smallest frame section to the middle-size section; then glue the middle-size section to the largest frame section. The painted edges of the middle section will be exposed around the frame and opening.

5. Cut a 5-inch (13cm) square of watercolor paper to fit behind the photo opening, and glue it to the back of the frame. Glue only on three sides so that the photo can be slipped into opening.

6. Using pattern provided opposite, cut one stand from watercolor paper. Fold at dotted line. Align the lower edge of the frame with bottom edge of stand. Glue only top section of stand to the back of the frame. To keep stand from spreading, cut a small length of ⅝-inch sheer ribbon and glue one end to the back of the frame and the other to the back of the stand.

7. Following General Bow Techniques on page 140, use the remaining ⅝-inch sheer ribbon to make a four-loop bow with streamers about 9 inches (23cm) long. Wire the center to hold. Glue bow to top center of frame.

8. Following General Bow Techniques, form two-loop bows using both sheer check ribbons; wire in the center to hold. Glue to center of first bow.

9. Following General Flower Techniques on page 139, make a gathered ribbon rose from 1½-inch sheer ribbon, and glue to center of bows.

10. Knot each streamer at two places and glue knots to sides of frame. Glue premade ribbon roses over knots. Cut ends of streamers into a "V."

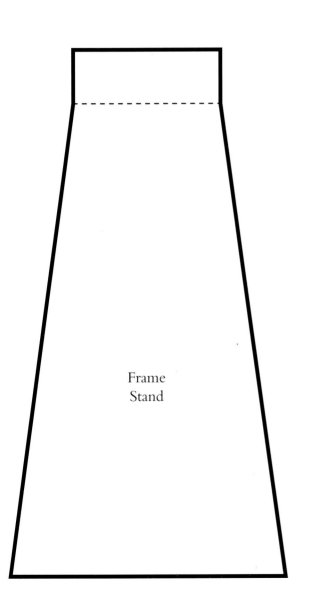

Frame
Stand

Baby's Keepsake Album

Make a pretty padded album to keep baby's pictures, birth announcements, congratulations cards, and other cherished mementos.

MATERIALS

1⅓ yds (1.3m) of ⅞-inch (2cm)-wide blue-and-white-striped ribbon

⅔ yd (61 cm) of 1½-inch (4 cm)-wide novelty ribbon in pink and white

⅝ yd (1.5m) of 1½ (4cm)-inch-wide pink-and-white-striped ribbon

⅔ yd (61 cm) of premade ribbon garland in blue

4 premade ribbon flowers in pink

4 premade ribbon flowers in white

9 x 14 inch (23 x 35.5cm) refillable photo album

5 x 7 inch (13 x 17.5cm) cardboard mat

½ yd (50cm) of white cotton brushed flannel fabric

½ yd (50cm) of fusible fleece

Poster board

DIRECTIONS

1. Unscrew posts that hold album together. Set aside pages and screws.

2. Cut fusible fleece to fit album front and back. Note that fleece should cover only front and back album sections and should not extend into the area where album sections are attached to pages. Following manufacturer's instructions, fuse fleece to album sections.

3. Cut a narrow strip of fusible fleece to fit side section of album. Fleece should not extend into the area where front and back sections are attached. Following manufacturer's instructions, fuse fleece to album side.

4. Cut flannel fabric to fit front and back album sections. Fabric must be approximately 1 inch (2.5cm) larger all around so that the fabric can be turned to the back of the sections and glued in place. Place wrong side of fabric against album section with fusible fleece. Bring raw fabric edges to back and glue to hold.

5. Cut flannel fabric to fit side section. Note that fabric should be cut 1 inch (2.5cm) larger at top and bottom so that it can be glued to the back of the section and no raw edges will show. Raw edges at sides will not show when album is assembled. Place wrong side of fabric against side section with fusible fleece. Glue sides down and bring raw edges to the back and glue to hold.

6. Measure inside front and back album covers and cut poster board to fit. Cut fabric to fit poster board, making sure it is about 1 inch (2.5cm) wider on all sides so that raw edges can be glued to back of boards. Glue fabric to poster boards.

7. Glue a length of premade ribbon garland and 1½-inch novelty ribbon to top and bottom of album front section. Raw edges of ribbon at front side are glued to the back of the section.

8. When all glued sections of album are dry, glue covered poster boards to front and back inside covers of album. Weigh with a few books and let glue dry completely.

9. When glue on all sections is dry, assemble the album.

10. Cut fusible fleece to fit cardboard mat. Following manufacturer's instructions, fuse fleece to mat.

11. Cut flannel fabric to fit mat, making sure it is about 1 inch (2.5cm) larger all around so raw edges can be glued to back of mat. Place wrong side of fabric against fleece. Bring raw edges around to back and glue. Cut out excess fabric at center of mat, leaving 1 inch extra to turn to the back and glue. Clip fabric at inside corners of mat. Turn raw edges to back of mat and glue.

12. Glue lengths of $^7/_8$-inch blue-and-white-striped ribbon to each side of the covered mat.

13. Glue covered mat to the center of album. Make sure the mat is glued only along three sides. The unglued side will create an opening so that a photo can be inserted behind the mat.

14. Glue ribbon flowers around mat.

15. Use $1^1/_2$-inch pink-and-white-striped ribbon to form a simple two-loop bow. Gather at the center with a few hand stitches. Glue to upper left of album.

16. Tie a two-loop bow with the remaining blue-and-white ribbon and glue to center of pink striped bow.

THE MOST POPULAR BABY NAMES
OF THE TWENTIETH CENTURY

1900		1950		1999	
GIRLS	**BOYS**	**GIRLS**	**BOYS**	**GIRLS**	**BOYS**
Mary	John	Linda	John	Emily	Jacob
Helen	William	Mary	James	Sarah	Michael
Anna	James	Patricia	Robert	Brianna	Matthew
Margaret	George	Barbara	William	Samantha	Nicholas
Ruth	Charles	Susan	Michael	Hailey	Christopher
Elizabeth	Joseph	Maria	David	Ashley	Joshua
Marie	Frank	Sandra	Richard	Kaitlyn	Austin
Rose	Henry	Nancy	Thomas	Madison	Tyler
Florence	Robert	Deborah	Charles	Hannah	Brandon
Bertha	Harry	Kathleen	Gary	Alexis	Joseph

Pocket Heart Favors

Wide ribbons woven together are filled with candies for a shower favor that is lovely to look at and fun to give.

MATERIALS for one favor

²/₃ yd (61 cm) of 2⅝-inch (6.5cm)-wide merrowed-wire-edge ribbon, cut into two equal lengths

1 yd (1m) of ribbon ⅜-inch (1cm) or wider

Assorted premade ribbon flowers

Potpourri or candy to fill heart

DIRECTIONS

1. Fold each length of 2⅝-inch-wide ribbon in half. Cut the open ends in a curved shape.

2. Cut two slits into folded edge, approximately 2¾-inch (7cm) up from folded edge.

(Directions continued on page 32)

3. Using illustration as a guide, weave the loops together by inserting loop 3 into loop 4. Pull loop 4 into loop 2. Insert loop 1 into 4.

4. For next row, pull loop 5 into loop 3. Insert loop 2 into loop 5 and pull loop 5 into loop 1.

5. Next row, insert loop 3 into loop 6. Pull loop 6 into loop 2 and insert loop 1 into loop 6.

6. Adjust loops.

7. Glue heart together at top and sides of curved edges.

8. Cut a 1-yard (1m) length of ribbon into two lengths. From one length, make a loop and glue it inside heart at front and back. Make decorative bow from other length and glue to front.

9. Glue premade ribbon roses to front.

10. Fill with a handful of potpourri or candies.

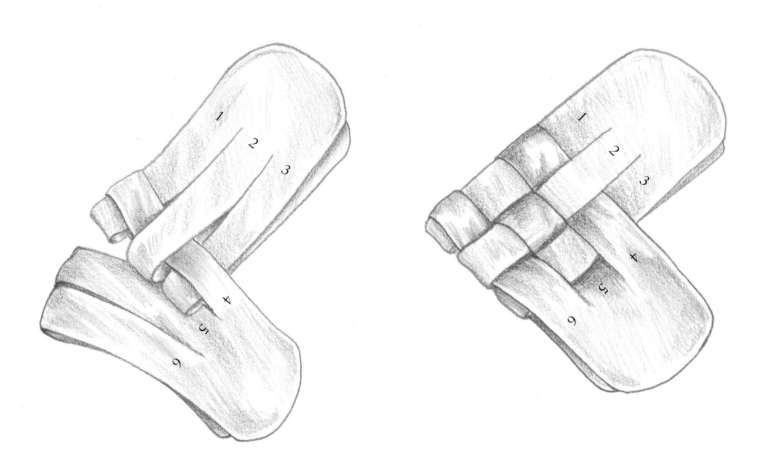

BABY SHOWER FUN

One popular trend at baby showers is for the guests to work on simple craft projects such as hand-decorating wooden or Lucite picture frames with ribbons and small ornaments. It's fun to have an activity at the shower, and the partygoers leave with a special memento to treasure.

Most of the items you'll need can be purchased inexpensively at crafts or fabric stores. Make sure to have on hand:

* Picture frames (one for each guest, plus an extra few in case any are accidentally broken)

* Several pairs of scissors

* Glue

* Paint and paintbrushes

* An assortment of ribbons and lace

* A variety of small bows, premade ribbon flowers, ribbon animals, small charms

A baby is an angel whose wings decrease as his legs increase.

—FRENCH PROVERB

Chapter Two

Baby's Homecoming

PART OF THE JOY OF WELCOMING a new baby is sharing the news with friends and family. The creative birth announcements in this chapter help spread the word, and make gorgeous mementos for the child to treasure as he or she grows. If the sex of the baby is not a surprise, the cards can be crafted in advance, with the baby's name, weight, date and time of birth, and other details left to be filled in after the birth. Otherwise, choose one of the announcements that doesn't specify boy or girl.

Once the baby is home, the important work of comforting and caring for him or her begins. For hundreds of years, mothers have rocked their babies to sleep in cradles made of leather, wood, wicker—even silver. The Greek philosopher Plato wrote of the benefits of rocking "for the bodies as well as the souls of the very young infants." During the Middle Ages, babies were rarely allowed to cry for fear of attracting the devil, so they were rocked almost continuously. Believe it or not, some professors and doctors felt that rocking was bad for the baby, asserting that "the blood and liquids stop in the head." This school of thought did not find great favor with mothers and baby nurses, however, and cradles and bassinets remain popular today for newborns.

The cradle in this chapter has special meaning for me, as it was my father's when he was a baby. I used it for my son, and my two grandchildren and my nephew all slept in it until they were about four months old. Here, it is outfitted with ruffles and ribbons for use by my granddaughter, Annabel Hope. The dust ruffle and bumpers were made from a Battenburg lace sheet; two sweet little pillows, designed to decorate a rocking chair, are made from lace-edged hand-kerchiefs. The pillows use satin ribbon threaded through the two layers to join them together.

I have also included a beautiful dress, perfect for a baptism, christening, or other blessing ceremony. In the past, when infant mortality was high, babies were often baptized within hours or days of their birth. The mother was not present, as she was recovering from childbirth. Neighbors came to visit the baby with offerings of food and this blessing, according to one source: "May God bless you and make you straight as a match, healthy as salt, full as an egg, sweet as sugar, and good as bread."

Children are likely to live up to what you believe of them.
—LADY BIRD JOHNSON

BABY ESSENTIALS

This list will get you started assembling the things you'll need for the new arrival. I'm sure you will add to it!

☆ Undershirts, gowns, stretchies, bibs, receiving blankets, booties, hats

☆ Baby bathtub, washcloths, baby wash, shampoo, lotion, baby wipes, burping cloths

☆ Bassinet and sheets, crib and sheets, bumpers, mattress pads, blankets, night light, glider chair or rocker, changing table, hamper, diaper genie, comb and brush set

☆ Infant car seat, carriage or stroller, diaper bag

☆ Teddy bear, photo album, cassette player and tapes, baby monitor

☆ Lots of diapers!

Just Arrived!
name
date
weight
parents

Ribbon-Embellished Birth Announcements

Make your own announcements using rubber stamps and ribbons, and then fill in the name of your new bundle of joy.

Baby Girl Gingham Ribbon Announcement

MATERIALS

1 yd (1m) of ⅝-inch (1.5cm)-wide gingham ribbon in light pink

1 premade ribbon aster in pink

4 x 5-inch (10 x 13cm) scallop-edged postcard

4½ x 5½-inch (11.5 x 14cm) pink paper

"Just Arrived" rubber stamp

Pink ink pad

Hole punch

DIRECTIONS

1. Ink the stamp and apply it to the center of the postcard.

2. Measure and mark twenty pencil dots about ¾ inch (2cm) apart around edge of postcard for placement of hole punches. Punch holes at dots.

3. Thread gingham ribbon through holes, beginning and ending at upper left corner of postcard. Tie ends into a two-loop bow.

4. Glue the ribbon aster to center of bow.

5. Glue postcard to pink paper.

Sheer Ribbon Rose Announcement

MATERIALS

⅝ yd (1.5m) of ⅜-inch (1cm)-
wide sheer ribbon in pink

5 premade small sheer ribbon roses
in pink

4½ x 5-inch (11.5 x 13cm) folded
note card

Birth announcement stamp

Light blue pigment ink

Clear embossing powder

Pastel pink and yellow markers

DIRECTIONS

1. Ink the stamp and apply it to the center of the card. Apply embossing powder and emboss following manufacturer's instructions.

2. Color the stamped image with markers.

3. Following General Bow Techniques on page 140, make a small four-loop bow with sheer ribbon, leaving streamers about 6 inches (15cm) long. Secure bow with a few stitches. Glue bow to upper left of stamped image. Glue one ribbon rose to center of bow.

4. Loop and glue streamers to card. Trim streamers. Glue remaining roses to streamers.

"It's a Girl" Announcement

MATERIALS

½ yd (50cm) of ¼-inch (6mm)-
wide double-face satin ribbon
in pink

4 premade small ribbon roses in
pink

4¼ x 5-inch (11.5 x 13cm) folded
card

"It's a Girl!" stamp

Pink pigment ink

Silver embossing powder

DIRECTIONS

1. Ink the stamp and apply it to the center of the card. Apply embossing powder and emboss following manufacturer's instructions.

2. Cut ribbon into four lengths and glue around stamped image, forming a frame. Note that ends of ribbon should be cut on the diagonal.

3. Glue ribbon roses to each corner of ribbon frame.

Baby Carriage Note Card

MATERIALS

¼ yd (23cm) of ¼-inch (6mm)-wide double-face satin ribbon in pink

½ yd (50cm) of ⅝-inch (1.5cm)-wide sheer ribbon in pink

3 premade small sheer ribbon roses in pink

3½ x 5-inch (9 x 13cm) folded note card with raised border

Baby carriage stamp

Pink pigment ink

Silver embossing powder

DIRECTIONS

1. Ink the stamp and apply it to the center of the card. Apply embossing powder and emboss following manufacturer's instructions.

2. Cut satin ribbon into two lengths to fit left top border of card. Cut ends of ribbon on the diagonal and glue in place.

3. Form sheer ribbon into small four-loop bow and secure with a few stitches. Glue bow to upper left of card where ribbons meet. Glue ribbon roses to center of bow.

HAPPY BIRTHDAY

The well-loved song "Happy Birthday to You," originally titled "Good Morning to You" was written in 1893 by Mildred and Patty Smith Hill, two sisters from Kentucky. The two were trained as schoolteachers by their progressive parents, and Patty became a pioneer in kindergarten education.

Baby Boy "Just Arrived" Announcement

MATERIALS

¼ yd (23cm) of ⅜-inch (1cm)-wide satin ribbon in blue

½ yd (50cm) of ⅝-inch (1.5cm)-wide sheer ribbon in blue

1 premade small ribbon rose in white

4¼ x 5½-inch (11.5 x 14cm) folded note card

"Just Arrived" rubber stamp

Handprint rubber stamp

Light blue ink

DIRECTIONS

1. Ink the "Just Arrived" stamp and apply it to the center of the card. Ink the handprint stamp and apply it to lower right of card.

2. Cut satin ribbon into two lengths and glue to left and top sides of card.

3. Following General Bow Techniques on page 140, make a small four-loop bow using the sheer ribbon. Glue bow to upper left side of card where ribbons meet. Glue ribbon rose to center.

Between the dark and the daylight,
  When the night is beginning to lower,
Comes a pause in the day's occupations
  That is known as the Children's Hour.

I hear in the chamber above me
  The patter of little feet,
The sound of a door that is opened,
  And voices soft and sweet.

From my study I see in the lamplight,
  Descending the broad hall-stair,
Grave Alice, and laughing Allegra,
  And Edith with golden hair.

A whisper, and then a silence:
  Yet I know by their merry eyes
They are plotting and planning together
  To take me by surprise.

—From *The Children's Hour*
HENRY WADSWORTH LONGFELLOW

"It's a Boy" Announcement

MATERIALS

3/4 yd (69cm) of 3/8-inch (1cm)-wide satin ribbon in blue

4 1/4 x 5 1/2-inch (11.4 x 14cm) folded note card

"It's a Boy!" rubber stamp

Light blue pigment ink

Blue pearl embossing powder

DIRECTIONS

1. Ink the stamp and apply it to the center of card. Apply embossing powder and emboss following manufacturer's instructions.

2. Cut two 6-inch (15cm) lengths of ribbon and two 4 3/4-inch (12 cm) lengths of ribbon. Cut the ends on an angle. Glue ribbons to sides of card, placing longer lengths closer to the center of the card. Note that excess ribbon is folded and glued to the back of the card.

3. Cut one 5-inch (8 cm) length of ribbon with ends cut on an angle. Glue ribbon across the top of the card about 5/8-inch (1.6cm) down from the fold.

Monday's child is fair of face,

Tuesday's child is full of grace,

Wednesday's child is full of woe,

Thursday's child has far to go,

Friday's child is loving and giving,

Saturday's child works hard for its living,

But the child that is born on the Sabbath day

Is bonny and blithe and good and gay.

—ANONYMOUS

Thank You Note

MATERIALS

½ yd (50cm) of ⅝-inch (1.5cm)-
   wide gingham ribbon in blue

1 folded note card, 4¼ x 5½-inch
   (11.5 x 14cm)

"Thank You" rubber stamp

Light blue ink

DIRECTIONS

1. Ink the stamp and apply to lower right side of card.

2. Cut a 6-inch (15cm) length of ribbon, cutting the ends of ribbon into a "V."
   Glue ribbon to left side of card. Note that excess ribbon is folded and glued
   to the back of the card.

3. Tie remaining ribbon into small two-loop bow. Glue bow onto the side
   ribbon, near the top of the card.

Baby Rattle Note Card

MATERIALS

⅔ yd (61 cm) of ⅝-inch (1.5cm)-
   wide gingham check ribbon
   in blue

3½ x 5-inch (9 x 13cm) folded
   note card with raised border

Baby rattle rubber stamp

Blue ink

Clear embossing powder

DIRECTIONS

1. Ink the stamp and apply it to the center of the card. Apply embossing powder
   and emboss following manufacturer's instructions.

2. Glue ribbon around border of card.

3. Use remaining ribbon to make a small two-loop bow. Glue bow to base of rattle.

Battenburg Cradle Accessories

Baby will sleep peacefully in a cradle outfitted with pretty Battenburg lace bumpers and dust ruffles.

Crib Bumper

MATERIALS

5¼ yds (5m) of ⅜-inch (1cm)-wide feather-edge satin ribbon in white

4 yds (4m) of ³⁄₁₆-inch (5mm) feather-edge satin ribbon in white

6 pkgs of premade ribbon asters in white

Battenburg sheets

2½ yds (2.5m) of 45-inch (1.2m)-wide fabric (or untrimmed sections of sheets)

High-loft quilt batting

Tissue paper

DIRECTIONS

Note: ½-inch (1.5cm) seam allowances unless otherwise noted.

1. Measure the width and height of each cradle wall. When measuring width of bumper, add 1 inch (2.5cm) to width measurement. When measuring height, add 1½ inches (4cm) to height dimension.

2. Using these measurements, draw a tissue paper pattern. Label pattern pieces: head, foot, and side.

3. Position each pattern on the sheet with the Battenburg design along proper edge. Cut sheet along three remaining sides. Cut one head, one foot, and two sides.

4. Trim 1 inch off one long edge of each paper pattern. Use these patterns to cut plain fabric and quilt batting. Cut two head pieces, two foot pieces, and four side pieces from plain fabric. Cut one head, one foot, and two sides from quilt batting.

5. To assemble bumper: Pin and stitch narrow feather-edge satin ribbon in V configuration on the right side of the Battenburg bumper, measuring approximately ½ inch (1.5cm) below center design and 2 inches (5cm) below design at side edges.

6. On each side edge of Battenburg bumper, clip fabric 1 inch down from design edge and ½ inch in from sides. Turn under and stitch a ¼-inch (6mm) double hem above clip.

7. Using two plain fabric bumper sections, pin and stitch right sides together on one long edge. Press seam open.

8. Position Battenburg bumper over right side of plain bumper with lower and side edges even. Pin in place along seams. Stitch Battenburg to the plain bumpers by top stitching in the ditch of the seam and basting along sides and lower edge.

9. Turn over plain bumper to meet lower and side edges of Battenburg bumper. Pin the three layers together. Position layers on quilt batting and pin again. Stitch the four layers together on lower and side edges, leaving an opening at bottom for turning. Turn right side out. Stitch opening closed.

10. Cut four 24-inch (61cm) lengths of $3/8$-inch ribbon. Stitch one end of ribbon to right side of bumper at each top corner and one end of each ribbon to wrong side of bumper at each bottom corner.

11. Stitch ribbon flowers to center of lace medallion and center area of each open triangle created by ribbon placement.

12. Repeat for each bumper section. Tie bumper sections together inside cradle.

Cradle Dust Ruffle

MATERIALS

Battenburg sheets

Narrow spring-tension curtain rods
   to fit cradle dimensions

Tissue paper

DIRECTIONS

1. For the cutting width of the dust ruffle, measure and multiply the measurement by 1.5. For cutting length of the ruffle, measure length and add 3 inches (7.5cm).

   Note: Our cradle had working mechanics at the head and foot, which prevented us from placing a dust ruffle in these locations. If your cradle allows, place a dust ruffle at foot and head as well as sides.

2. Using these measurements, draw a tissue paper pattern. Position the pattern on the sheet with the Battenburg design along one long edge. Cut the sheet along three remaining edges.

3. Fold under 1 inch (2.5cm) on side edges and press. Open the crease and fold raw edge under, creating a ½-inch (1.5cm) double hem. Stitch in place.

4. To create header at top: Turn under top raw edge ½ inch (1.5cm) to wrong side of fabric. Measuring from crease, fold top edges under 2½ inches (6.5cm). Stitch in place along original fold. Stitch again 1¼ inch (3cm) from stitching.

5. Slip rod through casing and position dust ruffle between the vertical posts on cradle.

White-on-White Pillows

These exquisite yet easy-to-make pillows are created from lace handkerchiefs threaded together with white satin ribbons.

Square Doily Pillow

MATERIALS

3 yds (3m) of ¼-inch (6mm)-wide double-face satin ribbon in white

4 premade ribbon flower clusters

Two 13-inch (33cm) square Battenburg doilies

Two 11-inch (28cm) squares of white fabric

Polyester fiberfill

DIRECTIONS

Note: ½-inch (1.5cm) seam allowances unless otherwise noted.

1. To make the pillow form, stitch together the 11-inch squares of plain fabric, right sides together, leaving a small opening for turning. Turn right side out. Stuff with polyeser fiberfill and stitch opening closed.

2. With right sides up, pin edges of doilies together, with the pillow form "sandwiched" between them.

3. Cut four 27-inch (69cm) lengths of ribbon. Pin a safety pin to one end of ribbon. Using pin as though it was a needle, weave ribbon through the lace trim of doilies, "sewing" them together. Start at one corner and end at next. Leave ribbon tails long.

4. Repeat for all four sides. Tie ribbon tails together in bows and stitch ribbon flowers to each corner.

Heart Doily Pillow

MATERIALS

2 yds (2m) of ¼-inch (6mm)
   double-face satin ribbon in
   white

1 pkg premade large ribbon roses
   in white

Two 18-inch (50cm) oval
   Battenburg place mats

Two 18-inch (50cm) squares of
   white fabric

Polyester fiberfill

Tissue paper

DIRECTIONS

Note: ½-inch (1.5cm) seam allowances unless otherwise stated.

1. Enlarge pattern provided on page 52 by 25 percent and make tissue pattern.
   Cut two heart shapes from white fabric.

2. Stitch together all edges of heart shape, right sides together, leaving opening for
   turning. Turn to right side. Stuff with polyester fiberfill. Stitch opening closed.

3. With right sides out, pin edges of placemats together, with the pillow form
   "sandwiched" between them. Pin a safety pin to one end of ribbon. Using
   safety pin as a needle, weave ribbon through lace trim of placemats, "sewing"
   the two together. Start and end at the center of one short end of placemat.
   Leave ribbon tails long.

4. Gather the placemats together, pulling gathers toward indent of heart form.
   Stitch gathers to form.

5. Tie ribbon tails together. Stitch ribbon roses to gathers.

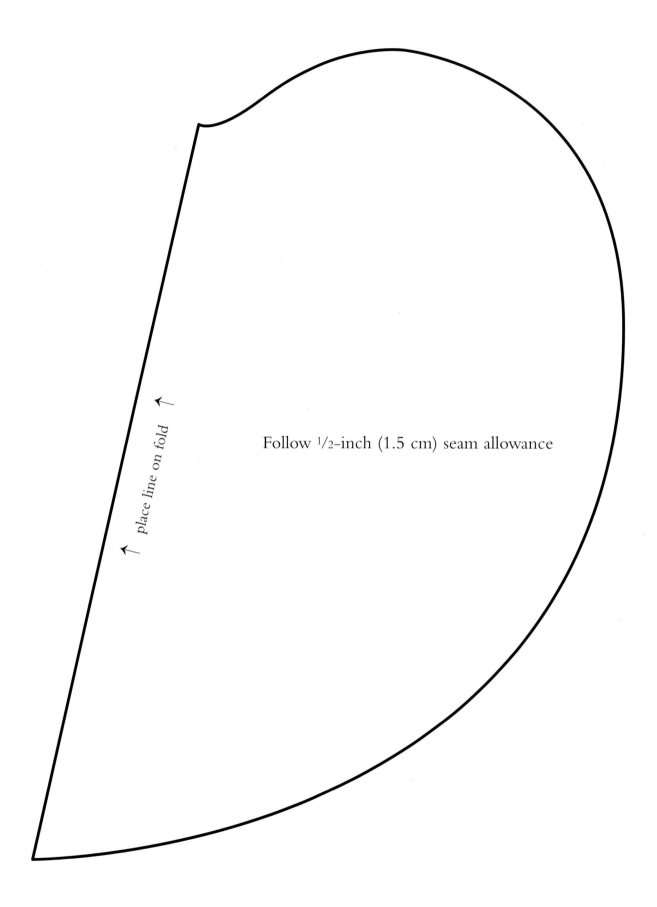

place line on fold

Follow ½-inch (1.5 cm) seam allowance

Know you what it is to be a child?

   It is to be something very different from
the man of today.
It is to have a spirit yet streaming from the
waters of Baptism;
   It is to believe in Love,
To believe in Loveliness,
   To believe in belief;
It is to be so little that the elves can reach to
whisper in your ear;
   It is to turn pumpkins into coaches, mice
      into horses, lowness into
      loftiness, and
      nothing into everything,
for each child has its Fairy Godmother
in its soul.

                    —PERCY BYSSHE SHELLEY

Heirloom Hankie Bonnet

A lace-trimmed handkerchief becomes baby's first bonnet and is then tucked away to become the "something old" for "baby's" wedding. Simply remove the stitches for the casing and the ribbon ties, and the bonnet is transformed back into a handkerchief.

MATERIALS

1¾ yds (1.75m) of ⅜-inch (1cm)-wide jacquard ribbon

1⅜ yds (1.6m) of 1½-inch (4cm)-wide jacquard ribbon

6 premade ribbon roses

11-inch (28cm) square laced-edged handkerchief

DIRECTIONS

1. Cut four 12-inch (30cm) lengths of ⅜-inch-wide ribbon. Cut one 12-inch length of 1½-inch-wide ribbon.

2. Measure in ½ inch (1.5cm) from one lace edge of handkerchief and stitch one ⅜-inch-wide ribbon length in place, turning under side edges. Stitch 1½-inch-wide ribbon length next to ⅜-inch-wide ribbon, turning under side edges. Stitch a length of ⅜-inch-wide ribbon along other edge of 1½-inch-wide ribbon. Fold this edge of lace handkerchief back to form hatband.

3. Cut remaining 1½-inch-wide ribbon in half to form bonnet ties. Slip other edge between hat and band. Stitch in place. Stitch roses to band where streamers are attached, stitching through all layers. Cut ends of ribbon on diagonal or in V-shape.

4. Space two lengths of ⅜-inch-wide ribbon along other edge of hankie, 2 inches (5cm) and 4 inches (10cm) from lace edge. Stitch in place.

5. Fold this lace edge back to form casing, with lace edge on outside of hat, and stitch. Thread remaining ⅜-inch-wide ribbon through casing, then gather and tie into bow.

Christening Gown and Bonnet

*T*his gown is sewn from a commercial pattern, but rows of ribbons make it special, creating an heirloom for generations to come.

Christening Gown

MATERIALS

3 yds (3m) of ⅞-inch (2cm)-wide lace-edged satin ribbon

4⅛ yds (4.1m) of ⅜-inch (1cm)-wide ribbon

2⅜ yds (2.58m) of ¾-inch (2cm)-wide ribbon

1½ yds (1.5m) of 4-inch (10cm) flat lace

Assorted premade ribbon flowers

1 yd (1m) sheer white fabric

Simplicity Pattern 7488 or other commercial pattern

Fabric and notions as stated in pattern

Ribbon for front bodice: 14-inch (35.5cm) lengths of assorted variety and widths of ribbons to measure width of bodice pattern piece—approximately 6 inches (15cm) wide, about 3 to 6 yds (3–5.5m) of ribbon

Ribbon for both sleeves: 35-inch (89cm) lengths of assorted variety and widths of ribbons to measure width of pattern sleeve—approximately 18 inches (50cm) wide. Yardage will vary greatly depending on choices; can be 12 yds (11m) to 24 yds (22m). May also insert fabric strips between ribbons.

Ribbon for skirt insertion: 6-inch (15cm) lengths of assorted variety and widths of ribbons to measure 51 inches (1.3m) wide. Yardage will vary greatly depending on choices; can range from 8 yds to 20 yds. May also insert fabric strips between ribbons.

DIRECTIONS

1. Follow Simplicity Pattern 7488 cutting and layout diagrams with these exceptions: Cut the sleeves, back yoke lining, front yoke, and lining pieces from the sheer fabric.

2. Following General Strip Piecing Techniques on page 141, use 35-inch (89cm) lengths of ribbons to create sleeves and 6-inch (15cm) lengths for creating skirt insertion panel. For front bodice, piece the ribbons horizontally instead of vertically as on sleeves and skirt.

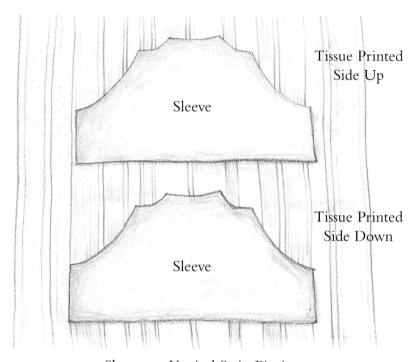

Sleeves on Vertical Strip Piecing

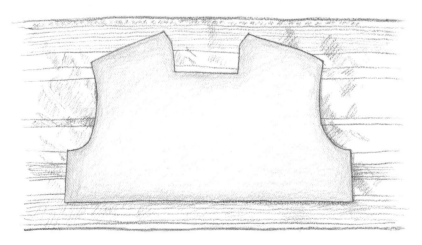

Bodice Yoke Front on Horizontal Strip Piecing

3. After yoke is cut from strip piecing, stitch right side of sheer fabric to wrong side of yoke. After sleeves are cut, stitch sheer lining and strip piecing with right sides together at lower hemline only. Turn right side out and press. Next, baste around outer edges.

4. Mark line across back yoke about 1 inch (2.5cm) below neck edge. Mark a second line about 1¾ inches (4.5cm) below first line. Check that lines on right back connect to lines on left back. On left back, place lower edge of ⅜-inch-wide ribbon on line, starting at armhole and proceeding to center back. At center back marking, fold over ribbon to create a point and return back across left back yoke butting edges (see illustration). Stitch in place. Repeat for second line. On right back, place one length of ⅜-inch-wide ribbon above line and one length below the line, butting edges. Check that they match up to left back and stitch. Repeat for second line.

To make point

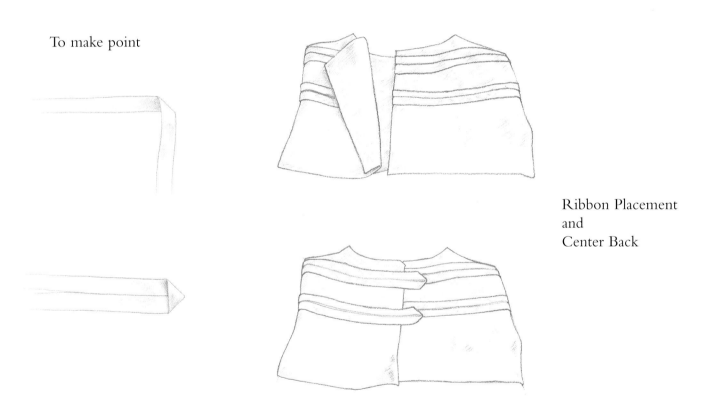

Ribbon Placement
and
Center Back

5. Stitch front to back at shoulders. Repeat for yoke lining. Stitch yoke to lining across center back seams and along neck edge. Clip, trim, and turn to right side. Press. Trim neck edge with ⅞-inch lace-edged satin ribbon. Stitch in place.

6. Trim hem of sleeves with ⅞-inch lace-edged satin ribbon. Stitch. Attach sleeves and finish yoke as instructed by pattern.

7. Attach skirt to yoke as instructed by pattern. Stitch a 28-inch (70cm) length of ⅜-inch ribbon to ¾-inch ribbon. Stitch one edge only around yoke front and back at lower edge just above seam line, turning under ribbon ends. Ribbons will hang below yoke and cover seam.

8. Measure and mark a line around skirt 10½ inches (27cm) above lower edge. Cut along line and set aside lower section. With right sides together, pin 6-inch (15cm) strip piecing insertion panel along this lower edge. Stitch. Press seam up. Stitch a length of ⅞-inch lace-edge satin ribbon on seam line.

9. Stitch lower section of skirt to lower edge of insertion panel. Press seam down. Form two 2-inch (5cm) pleats on lower section. Stitch 4-inch flat lace to hem. Stitch remaining length of ⅜-inch ribbon to ¾-inch ribbon. Stitch two ribbons on one edge only to lower seam line of insertion panel, turning under ends of ribbons.

10. Finish as instructed by pattern. Add premade ribbon roses as desired.

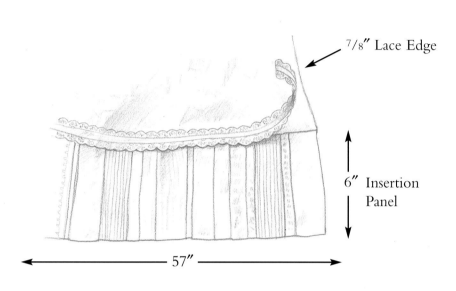

⅞″ Lace Edge

6″ Insertion Panel

57″

Attaching Insertion Panel to Skirt

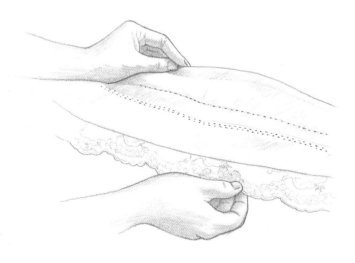

Attach Lace to Hem at Lower Edge of Pleating

STORING BABY'S CHRISTENING GOWN

To store your baby's gown for future generations, wash it first with a gentle detergent and allow it to air-dry. Fold the gown with acid-free tissue paper between the folds and place in a cotton bag (a pillowcase will do). Occasionally, remove the gown and refold it to prevent damaging creasing.

When the first baby laughed for the first time, the laugh broke into a thousand pieces and they all went skipping about, and that was the beginning of fairies.

— J.M. BARRIE

Christening Bonnet

MATERIALS

2 yds (2m) of ³/₄-inch (2cm)-wide ribbon, cut into four equal lengths

1½ yds (1.5m) of 1½-inch (4cm)-wide picot-edge sheer stripe ribbon

1½ yds (1.5m) of ⁷/₈-inch (2cm)-wide lace-edge satin ribbon

1½ yds (1.5m) of ⁷/₈-inch (2cm)-wide sheer stripe ribbon

½ yd (50cm) of ³/₈-inch (1cm)-wide jacquard ribbon

½ yd (50cm) of ³/₈-inch (1cm)-wide feather-edge ribbon

1 yd (1m) of ³/₄-inch (2cm)-wide feather-edge ribbon, cut in half

½ yd (50cm) of sheer fabric for lining and casing

Assorted premade ribbon flowers

DIRECTIONS

Note: Bonnet uses same basic combination of ribbons as dress yoke.

1. Following General Strip Piecing Techniques on page 141, piece 14-inch (35.5cm) lengths of ³/₄-inch-wide ribbon, ⁷/₈-inch sheer stripe ribbon, ⁷/₈-inch lace-edge satin ribbon, ³/₄-inch-wide ribbon, 1½-inch sheer stripe ribbon, and another length of ³/₄-inch-wide ribbon to form bonnet base.

2. Sew remaining lengths of ⁷/₈-inch sheer ribbon and 1½-inch sheer stripe ribbon together along one edge. Make a running stitch along edge of ribbons and pull up to gather. Finish ends of ribbons.

3. To form casing section, make ½-inch (1.5cm) hem on side edges. Fold section in half to measure 2½ inches (6.5cm). Stitch ½ inch (1.5cm) from fold to form casing. Pin to right side of bonnet back. Stitch. Insert ³/₈-inch feather-edge ribbon through casing and tie in bow.

4. Hem one long edge of bonnet lining. With right sides together, pin lining to bonnet, sandwiching casing between lining and bonnet. Stitch side edges. Turn right side out.

5. Stitch length of ³/₈-inch jacquard ribbon to length of ³/₄-inch ribbon. Turn ends under. Stitch ribbons on one edge only to back seam, catching lining in stitching to hold in place.

6. Zigzag to attach ruffle to front of bonnet and lining.

7. Edge in ⁷/₈-inch lace-edge satin ribbon; attach ties and premade ribbon roses.

"Sugar and Spice" Bibs ⟋⟍

*P*iece rows of ribbons together and trim with ribbon roses for exquisite baby bibs.

M A T E R I A L S for
White-on-White Bib

2/3 yd (61cm) of 5/8-inch (1.5cm)-
  wide feather-edge satin ribbon
  in white, cut in half

3/4 yd (69cm) of 1 1/2-inch (4cm)-
  wide textured ribbon in white

1 1/3 yds (1.3m) of 5/8-inch (1.5cm)-
  wide floral ribbon in white

1 2/3 yds (1.3m) of 3/8-inch (1cm)-
  wide floral ribbon in white

6 premade sheer roses in white

2 premade small satin roses in white

1 leaf green embroidery floss

1/3 yd (30.5cm) of off-white cotton
  fabric

M A T E R I A L S for
Pink Calico Bib

3/4 yd (69cm) of 1/4-inch (6mm)-
  wide grosgrain ribbon in pink

3/4 yd (69cm) of 3/8-inch (1cm)-
  wide feather-edge satin ribbon
  in pink (for ties)

5/8 yd (1.5m) of 7/8-inch (2cm)-
  wide lace edged satin ribbon
  in pink and white

7/8 yd (80cm) of 3/4-inch (2cm)-
  wide jacquard ribbon in pink

3/4 yd (69cm) of 1 1/2-inch (4cm)-
  wide textured ribbon in mauve

6 premade small satin roses in
  light pink

2 premade large satin roses in
  light pink

White embroidery floss

1/3 yd (30.5cm) of cotton fabric in
  pink and white floral print

DIRECTIONS

Note: $1/4$-inch (6mm) seam allowances unless otherwise stated.

1. Prewash the cotton fabric, then dry and iron it. Using pattern included on page 68, cut two bib pieces.

2. **For White-on-White Bib:** Cut two 10-inch (25.5cm) lengths of $1\frac{1}{2}$-inch-wide ribbon. Stitch $5/8$-inch floral ribbon to both sides of $1\frac{1}{2}$-inch ribbon lengths. Using 6-inch (15cm) length of remaining $1\frac{1}{2}$-inch ribbon, stitch $3/8$-inch floral ribbon to both sides. Stitch ribbons to the bib using illustration opposite as a guide. Stitch $5/8$-inch feather-edge ribbon between ribbon strips. **For Pink Calico Bib:** Cut a 6-inch (15cm) length of $1\frac{1}{2}$-inch ribbon. Stitch a length of $3/4$-inch jacquard ribbon to both sides of ribbon length. Cut remaining length of $1\frac{1}{2}$-inch ribbon in half. Stitch a length of $3/4$-inch ribbon to opposite sides of $1\frac{1}{2}$-inch ribbon lengths. Stitch ribbons to the bib using photograph as guide. Stitch lace-edged satin ribbon between ribbon strips.

3. With the right sides together, stitch front and back bib sections together, leaving a 4-inch (10cm) opening for turning.

4. Trim and clip seam allowances. Turn the bib right side out. Press. Hand-stitch opening closed.

5. Following instructions on page 140, embellish bib edges with buttonhole stitch.

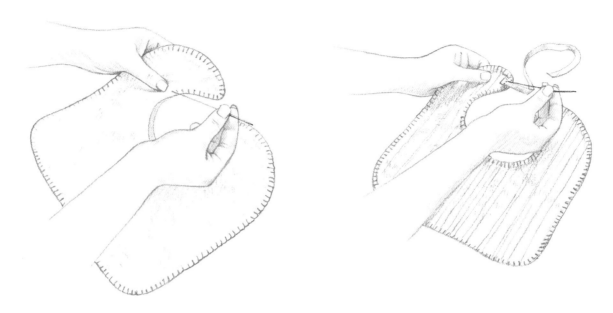

6. Cut two 13$\frac{1}{4}$-inch (33.5cm) lengths of ribbons for bib ties ($\frac{3}{8}$-inch floral for white bib and $\frac{1}{4}$-inch pink grosgrain for calico bib). Fold under $\frac{1}{2}$ inch (1.5cm) on one end and stitch to end of neck opening, as illustrated.

7. Stitch a small ribbon rose on top of the bib tie to cover the previous stitching.

8. Stitch three premade ribbon roses in each of the front corners of the bib. (The pink calico bib will have one large and two small roses in each corner; the white-on-white bib will have three sheer satin roses in each corner.)

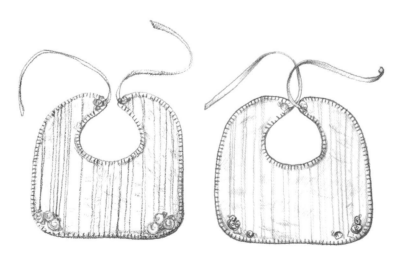

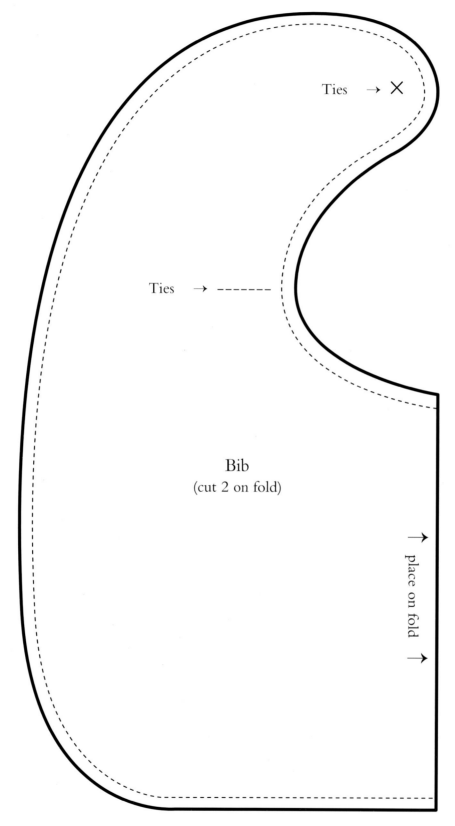

Ties → ✕

Ties → -------

Bib
(cut 2 on fold)

→
place on fold
→

Enlarge pattern by 20 percent

BIRTH MONTH LORE

Gemstones and flowers have long been associated with particular months, and gifts incorporating these stones and blossoms, or their colors, make meaningful presents for the new baby.

MONTH	BIRTHSTONE	FLOWER
JANUARY	Garnet	Carnation
FEBRUARY	Amethyst	Violet
MARCH	Aquamarine	Jonquil
APRIL	Diamond	Sweet Pea
MAY	Emerald	Lily-of-the-Valley
JUNE	Pearl	Rose
JULY	Ruby	Larkspur
AUGUST	Peridot	Gladiolus
SEPTEMBER	Sapphire	Aster
OCTOBER	Opal	Calendula
NOVEMBER	Topaz	Chrysanthemum
DECEMBER	Turquoise	Narcissus

Chapter Three

Sweet Dreams
Decorating the Nursery

Decorating the new baby's room is an act of love for the new parents. Knowing the sex of the baby in advance can help guide the choices of colors and patterns used in this very special room. The two nursery ensembles featured in this chapter started with the same commercial pattern but use very different patterns and color schemes. With a few adjustments, either motif could be used for a boy or a girl.

Offray ribbons were the starting point for each of these themed nurseries—the "Noah's Ark" theme uses soft pastel lavender, mint, and yellow ribbons to create a dreamy atmosphere. Although the accessories shown here are finished with a feminine eyelet ruffle, this detail could easily be eliminated for a boy. The "Bear Goes Fishing" theme features brighter colors, blue denim, and a cozy plaid. As the baby grows, simply remove the lower dust ruffle to accommodate the change in the crib's mattress position. The bumpers are reversible and are easy to make using a new batting designed especially for this purpose. Additional accents for the nursery include pillows, window treatments, diaper bags, and lamp shades.

"Noah's Ark" Nursery Ensemble

Softly colored ribbons depicting Noah's Ark combine with pretty pastel fabrics for a light and airy nursery. Enlarging the Noah's Ark motif on the ribbon personalizes the quilt and headboard decoration. Pillows for Mom's rocking chair continue the theme of baby's pastel nursery, while the coordinating diaper stacker, made with a commerical pattern and colorful ribbons, stores a ready supply of diapers. A pretty ribbon-trimmed lamp shade completes the ensemble in the Noah's Ark baby nursery.

To make the entire nursery, the following amounts of fabric, ribbons, eyelet trim, piping, and batting were used:

$5\frac{1}{2}$ yds (5m) of 45-inch (1.2m)–wide fabric in four coordinating colors

$22\frac{3}{4}$ yds (21m) of $1\frac{1}{2}$-inch (4cm)–wide plaid ribbon

$5\frac{3}{4}$ yds (5.5m) of $\frac{7}{8}$-inch (2cm)–wide baby print ribbon

$17\frac{1}{2}$ yds (16m) of $\frac{3}{8}$-inch (1cm)–wide plaid ribbon

5 yds (4.5m) of $\frac{3}{8}$-inch (1cm)–wide satin ribbon

9 yds (9m) of $\frac{3}{8}$-inch (1cm)–wide satin ribbon in coordinating color

$5\frac{1}{8}$ yds (5m) of $1\frac{1}{2}$-inch (4cm)–wide "Noah's Ark" printed ribbon

$2\frac{1}{2}$ yds (2.5m) of $\frac{7}{8}$-inch (2cm)–wide gingham ribbon

$7\frac{1}{8}$ yards (7m) of narrow piping

6 yds (6m) of 45-inch (1.2m)–wide eyelet fabric

1 package of quilt batting

1 package of bumper batting

$16\frac{3}{4}$ yds (15.3m) of 3-inch (7.5m)–wide pregathered eyelet trim

$2\frac{1}{2}$ yds (2.5m) of 18-inch (50cm) or slightly wider eyelet fabric

Fusible web

Crib Bumper

MATERIALS

9³⁄₈ yds (9m) of 1¹⁄₂-inch (4cm)-wide plaid ribbon in pastels

4 yds (4m) of ⁷⁄₈-inch (2cm)-wide novelty satin ribbon in pastels

4 yds (4m) of 3¹⁄₂-inch (9cm)-wide gathered eyelet trim

4 yds (4m) of piping

1 pkg bumper batting 10 inches wide x 15 feet long (25.5cm x 4.5m)

Simplicity Pattern #7674 or other commercial pattern

4 yds (4m) each of three coordinating fabrics. *Note:* Fabric should be cut along length of fabric; remaining widths of fabrics may be used for the headboard and quilt

Thread to match

DIRECTIONS

Note: Use ¹⁄₂-inch (1.5cm) seams throughout. Sew all fabrics right side together.

1. Cut backing fabric from pattern pieces as instructed by Simplicity pattern.

2. Cut remaining two fabrics into 4¹⁄₂ x 145-inch (11.5cm x 3.7m) lengths. Stitch together to form an 8 x 145-inch (20cm x 3.7m) length. Press seam open.

3. Center gathered eyelet edge over seam. Stitch in place.

4. Place ⁷⁄₈-inch-wide ribbon over eyelet edge. Stitch ribbon in place.

5. Stitch piping to upper edge of bumpers.

6. Cut 1¹⁄₂-inch plaid ribbons into twelve 28-inch (70cm) lengths. Fold in half and attach to bumper according to markings on Simplicity pattern.

7. Construct and finish bumper according to Simplicity pattern directions.

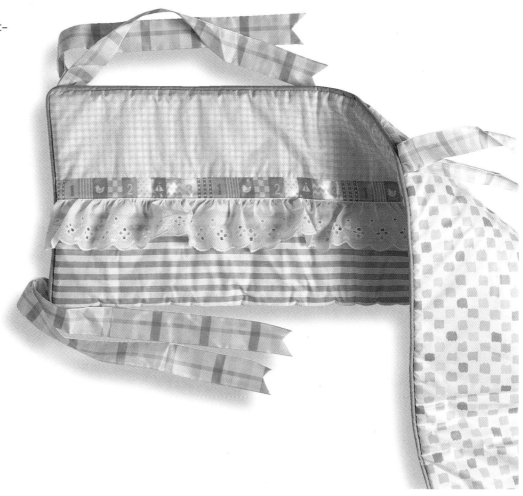

Dust Ruffles

MATERIALS for Short Dust Ruffle

11 yds (10m) of ⅜-inch (1cm)-wide plaid ribbon in pastels

Simplicity Pattern #7674 or other commercial pattern

Lavender fabric as required by pattern

MATERIALS for Long Dust Ruffle

⅜-inch (1cm)-wide ribbon for bows

Simplicity Pattern #7674 or other commercial pattern

45-inch (1.2m)-wide eyelet cotton fabric (double the amount specified on pattern envelope); long dust ruffle depth is increased to 20 inches (51cm) from 10 inches (25.5cm) on short dust ruffle.

DIRECTIONS

1. For short dust ruffle, cut out lavender fabric according to pattern pieces. Construct according to pattern directions. Hem as instructed.

2. Topstitch ⅜-inch pastel plaid ribbon around finished hem on all sides.

3. For long dust ruffle, use Simplicity pattern pieces and increase depth of ruffle to 20 inches (51cm) (or correct length for desired crib). Assemble following Simplicity pattern instructions.

4. Using 12-inch (30cm) lengths of ribbon, attach bows randomly to eyelets on dust ruffle.

5. Layer short dust ruffle on top of long dust ruffle for the finished look.

Crib Headboard Decoration

MATERIALS

5 yds (4.5m) of $3/8$-inch (1cm)-wide satin ribbon in yellow

$1^3/4$ yds (1.75m) of $1^1/2$-inch (4cm)-wide novelty print ribbon in blue

$2^1/2$ yds (2.5m) of piping

$2^1/2$ yds (2.5m) of 3-inch (7.5cm)-wide eyelet lace

Simplicity Pattern #7674 or other commercial pattern

Fabric, lining, and batting as required by pattern

16 x 16-inch (41 x 41cm) fabric piece for center applique

Fabric pieces for applique (8 to 10 12-inch [30cm] squares)

Fabric paints

Thread to match

Fusible web

DIRECTIONS

1. Following Simplicity pattern instructions, cut out fabric, lining, and batting. Using patterns included on pages 80–81, cut out appliques for center.

2. Using photo as a guide, place applique pieces on center insert. Thread length of $1^1/2$-inch novelty print ribbon through portholes of ship. Following General Instructions for Applique Work on page 140, applique in place. Use fabric paint to trace outlines and faces on each piece.

3. Center the insert panel in middle of headboard piece. Stitch in place.

4. Using $1^1/2$-inch novelty print ribbon, cover raw edges of insert panel. Stitch ribbon in place.

5. Attach piping then eyelet around outer edges of headboard piece. Lace $3/8$-inch ribbon through eyelet holes on trim.

6. Continue constructing headboard piece according to Simplicity pattern.

Baby Quilt

MATERIALS

3 yds (3m) of 1½-inch (4cm)-wide
novelty print ribbon in blue

1¾ (1.75m) yds of ⅞-inch (2cm)-
wide novelty print ribbon in
pastels

4½ yds (4.5m) of 1½-inch (4cm)-
wide plaid ribbon in pastels

4½ yds (4.5m) of ⅞-inch (2cm)-
wide gingham ribbon in yellow

6 yds (5.5m) of 3-inch (7.5cm)-
wide pregathered eyelet lace

9 yds (8.3m) of ⅜-inch (1cm)-
wide satin ribbon in lavender
(laced through eyelet)

Simplicity Pattern #7674 or other
commercial pattern

Fabric, lining, and batting as
required by pattern

14 x 17-inch (35.5 x 43cm) fabric
center for applique

24 x 30-inch (56 x 76cm) fabric
insert for quilt center

Fabric pieces for applique work
(8 to 10 12-inch [30cm] squares)

Fabric paints

Thread to match

Fusible web

DIRECTIONS

1. Following Simplicity pattern directions, cut out fabric, lining, and batting. Using patterns included on pages 80–81, cut out appliques for center work.

2. Using photo as a guide, place applique pieces on center insert. Thread length of 1½-inch novelty print ribbon through portholes of ship. Following General Instructions for Applique Work on page 140, applique in place. Use fabric paint to trace outlines and faces on each piece.

3. Center applique panel in middle of quilt insert panel. Stitch in place. Center this panel in middle of quilt front. Stitch in place.

4. Stitch 3-inch eyelet lace around edges of applique center panel. Place ⅞-inch novelty print ribbon around edges of panel, covering all raw edges of panel and eyelet trim. Stitch in place.

5. Using 1½-inch novelty print ribbon, cover raw edges of outer center panel. Stitch ribbon in place.

6. Stitch eyelet around outer edges of front quilt. Lace ⅜-inch ribbon through eyelet holes on all eyelet trim.

7. Continue constructing quilt according to pattern. Stitch ⅞-inch gingham ribbon to outer edges of quilt back. Stitch 1½-inch plaid ribbon to outer edges of quilt front. Stitch around edges of all ribbons on quilt front.

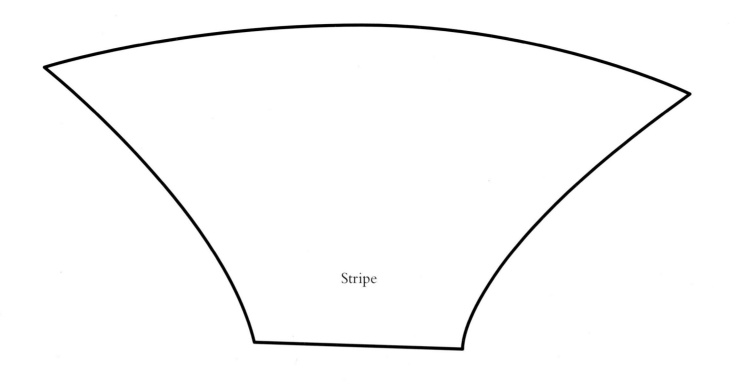

Stripe

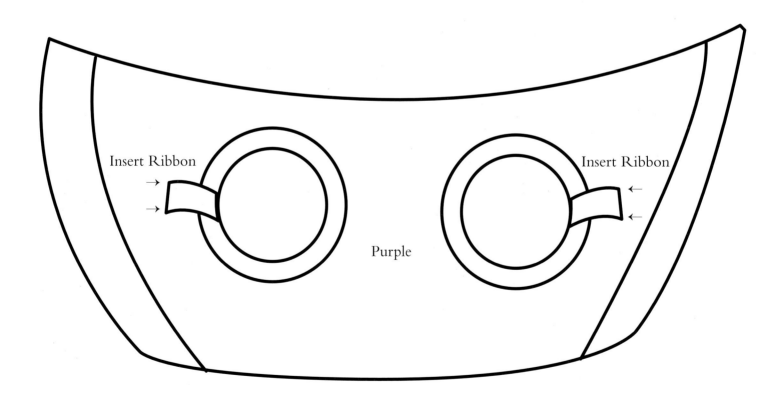

Insert Ribbon

Insert Ribbon

Purple

Enlarge pattern pieces by 20 percent

Blue

Peach

cut

Yellow

Yellow

cut → ← cut

Purple

Enlarge pattern pieces by 20 percent

Valance

MATERIALS

4 yds (4m) of ³⁄₈-inch (1cm)-wide plaid ribbon in pastels

5¹⁄₂ yds (5m) 1¹⁄₂-inch (4cm)-wide plaid ribbon in pastels

1³⁄₈ yds (1.6m) of fabric

2¹⁄₂ yds (2.5m) of eyelet fabric, 18 inches (50cm) or wider

DIRECTIONS

Note: All seams ¹⁄₂-inch (1.5cm) unless otherwise noted. Stitch right sides together.

1. Cut fabric into two 23-inch (58.5cm) lengths. Seam fabric together to form one piece. Narrow hem both side edges and lower edge of valance.

2. Stitch ³⁄₈-inch ribbon along the side and lower edges of valance.

3. Fold under 4¹⁄₂ inches (11.5cm) at upper edge of valance. Turn raw edge under ¹⁄₂ inch (1.5cm) to form hem. Pin along folded edge of hem.

4. Narrow hem side edges of eyelet fabric. With right side of eyelet facing up, tuck upper raw edge of eyelet fabric under hem fold. Stitch in place.

5. On right side of valance, place 1¹⁄₂-inch plaid ribbon along stitching for casing hem. Pin in place.

6. Cut two 18-inch (50cm) lengths of 1¹⁄₂-inch plaid ribbon. Use lengths to form a loop, 12 inches (30cm) in from both side edges of valance. Tuck raw edges of ribbon under ribbon and hem at casing. Stitch ribbon in place, forming casing.

7. Following General Bow Techniques on page 140, form two bows from remaining length of plaid ribbon. Stitch bows to valance where ribbon casing meets valance hem.

HOW TO SAY "I LOVE YOU"

In every part of the world and throughout time, babies have been welcomed with great joy and love. Here are the words parents around the globe use to tell their babies they love them.

Moi oiy neya	CANTONESE
Jeg elsker dig	DANISH
Ik hou van jou	DUTCH
Mahal ka ta	FILIPINO
Je t'aime	FRENCH
Ta gra agam ort	GAELIC
Ich liebe dich	GERMAN
Asavakit	GREENLANDIC
Ti amo	ITALIAN
Kimi o ai shiteru	JAPANESE
Ja cie kocham	POLISH
Ya vas liubliu	RUSSIAN
Te amo	SPANISH
Naku penda	SWAHILI
Mahal kita	TAGALOG
Mena Tanda Wena	ZULU

Square Pillow

MATERIALS

$1\frac{1}{2}$ yds (1.5m) of $\frac{3}{8}$-inch (1cm)-
wide plaid ribbon in pastels

$2\frac{1}{2}$ yds (2.5m) of $\frac{7}{8}$-inch (2cm)-
wide gingham ribbon in yellow

$1\frac{1}{4}$ yds (1.25m) of 3-inch (7.5cm)-
wide pregathered eyelet trim

$\frac{1}{2}$ yd (50cm) of fabric

10-inch (25.5cm) pillow form

Water soluble pen or disappearing
ink marker

DIRECTIONS

1. From fabric, cut one 15-inch (38cm) square for pillow front, one 10 x 15-inch (25.5 x 38cm) rectangle and one 13 x 15-inch (33 x 38cm) rectangle for pillow back pieces.

2. On pillow front piece, measure in 2 inches (5cm) from outside edges and mark with pen. Baste eyelet trim along markings, ruffled edge facing out to pillow edge.

3. Pin $\frac{7}{8}$-inch gingham ribbon to edge of eyelet, covering edge and mitering corners. Stitch inside edge only of ribbon at this time.

4. On pillow back fabric pieces, make hem along one edge of 10-inch side, and one edge of 13-inch side by folding under $\frac{1}{2}$ inch (5cm); press, fold under again, and stitch.

5. Overlap hemmed edges of fabric back pieces to form 15-inch square. Stitch together across top and bottom edges of fabric.

6. Stitch pillow front to back, right sides together. Trim corners, turn to right side. Press outside edges flat.

7. Stitch $\frac{3}{8}$-inch-wide plaid ribbon to outer edge of pillow.

8. Stitch outer edge of $\frac{7}{8}$-inch-wide ribbon, stitching through both front and back layers.

9. Cut remaining $\frac{7}{8}$-inch-wide ribbon into four equal lengths. Make two-loop bows and stitch to inside corners of eyelet.

Rectangular Pillow

MATERIALS

1³/₄ yds (1.75m) of 1¹/₂-inch (4cm)-wide plaid ribbon in pastel colors

2 yds (2m) of 3-inch (7.5cm)-wide pregathered eyelet trim

¹/₂ yd (50cm) of fabric in two coordinating colors

12 x 16-inch (30 x 40.5cm) pillow form

DIRECTIONS

1. From two fabrics, cut one piece each 7 x 17 inches (18 x 43cm) for pillow front, and from one fabric, cut one piece 13 x 17 inches (33 x 43cm) for pillow back.

2. Stitch two front pieces together along one 17-inch side to create a 13 x 17-inch rectangle.

3. On right side of pillow front, baste eyelet trim. Pin and stitch ribbon over edge of eyelet trim.

4. Pin and stitch eyelet trim to outer edge of pillow top, right side together.

5. Pin front to back, right sides together. Stitch, leaving opening to turn. Trim corners and turn to right side.

6. Insert pillow and hand stitch closed.

7. Cut remaining ribbon into two lengths. Make two bows and stitch to pillow front.

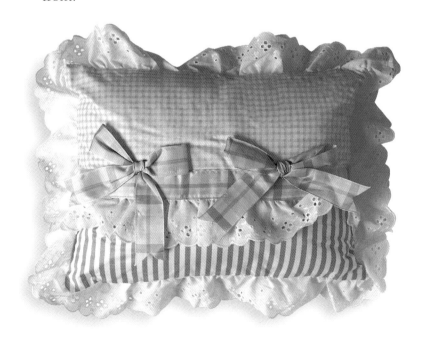

Lamp Shade

MATERIALS

2¾ yds (2.7m) of ⅜-inch (1cm)-wide satin ribbon in lavender

1¾ (1.74m) yds of ⅜-inch (1cm)-wide satin ribbon in yellow

1⅝ yds (1.75m) of eyelet beading trim

⅝ yd (58cm) of 2-inch (5cm)-wide pregathered eyelet trim

½ yd (50cm) of fabric

Glue

1 purchased self-adhesive lamp shade kit (kit used here was for a shade measuring 8 inches [20cm] high and 11 inches [28cm] across bottom edge)

DIRECTIONS

1. Following manufacturer's instructions, trace pattern on fabric and cut. Affix fabric to lamp shade as instructed.

2. Cut eyelet beading into a 1-yard (1m) length and thread length of lavender ribbon through eyelet openings. Thread yellow ribbon through the remaining length of eyelet beading.

3. Thread remaining lengths of ribbon through openings in 2-inch-wide pre-gathered eyelet trim.

4. Glue eyelet beading with lavender ribbon to bottom edge of shade.

5. Glue 2-inch eyelet trim to upper edge of shade, then layer eyelet beading with yellow ribbon over edge of eyelet trim.

Diaper Stacker

MATERIALS

1³/₈ yds (1.6m) of 1¹/₂-inch (4cm)-
wide plaid ribbon in pastels

³/₈ yd (34.5cm) of 1¹/₂-inch (4cm)-
wide novelty print ribbon

⁷/₈ yd (80cm) of ³/₈-inch (1cm)-
wide plaid ribbon in pastels

⁷/₈ yd (80cm) of 3-inch (7.5cm)-
wide pregathered eyelet trim

⁷/₈ yd (80cm) of piping

9 x 12-inch (23 x 30cm) piece of
¹/₄-inch (6mm) foamcore board

12 x 13-inch (30 x 33cm) piece of
quilt batting (remnant from quilt
and valances)

¹/₂ yd (50cm) of two coordinating
fabrics (remnants from other
projects)

Simplicity Pattern #7674 or other
commercial pattern

Thread to match

Coat hanger

DIRECTIONS

1. Using Simplicity pattern, cut out fabrics as directed, using photo as a guide.

2. Assemble stacker according to Simplicity pattern instructions with the following variations: After basting batting to stacker top front, attach piping around
lower edges. Stitch eyelet to lower edge below piping. Topstitch 1¹/₂-inch
novelty ribbon above piping on front only.

3. Stitch ³/₈-inch ribbon along front opening edges of stacker. Complete according
to Simplicity pattern instructions.

4. Cut two 24-inch (61cm) lengths of 1¹/₂-inch plaid ribbon; following General
Bow Techniques on page 140, make a bow from each. Attach to stacker as
shown.

5. Insert coat hanger in top opening. Insert 9 x 12-inch piece of foamcore into
bottom of stacker for stability.

"Bear Goes Fishing" Nursery Ensemble

*T*his lively nursery ensemble combines denim, plaids, and brightly colored ribbons for a playful air. The bear motif from the featured ribbon has been enlarged to serve as the central design in the adorable quilt. For a finished look, accent the nursery with additional ribbon-trimmed items like the lamp shade and a colorful wastebasket.

To make entire nursery, the following amounts of fabric and items were used:

5 yds (4.5m) of 54-inch (1.4m)-wide denim

5 yds (4.5m) of 45-inch (1.2m)-wide red polka-dot fabric

5 yds (4.5m) of 45-inch (1.2m)-wide navy striped fabric

10 to 12 yds (9–11m) of 45-inch (1.2m)-wide cotton plaid (extra for matching plaids)

One 40 x 60-inch (1 x 1.5m) piece of $^{1}/_{4}$-inch (6mm) foamcore board

81 x 96-inch (2 x 2.4m) quilt batting

Ribbons for entire nursery:

20 yds (18m) of $^{7}/_{8}$-inch (2cm)-wide grosgrain ribbon in red

13$^{1}/_{2}$ yds (12.5m) of $^{7}/_{8}$-inch (2cm)-wide satin ribbon "Crayola® Color Fun"

11$^{1}/_{2}$ yds (10.5m) of 1$^{1}/_{2}$-inch (4cm)-wide satin ribbon "Toybox" by Gear®

7$^{1}/_{2}$ yds (7m) of $^{5}/_{8}$-inch (1.5cm)-wide single-face satin ribbon in yellow-gold

7 yds (6.4m) of $^{3}/_{8}$-inch (1cm)-wide grosgrain ribbon in blue

7 yds (6.4m) of $^{1}/_{4}$-inch (6mm)-wide single-face satin ribbon in forest gren

12$^{1}/_{8}$ yds (11m) of $^{1}/_{4}$-inch (6mm)-wide single-face satin ribbon in yellow-gold

12$^{5}/_{8}$ yds (11.5m) of $^{3}/_{8}$-inch (1cm)-wide grosgrain ribbon in red

4$^{3}/_{4}$ yds (4.3m) of $^{7}/_{8}$-inch (2cm)-wide Train ribbon by Gear®

2$^{1}/_{2}$ yds (2.5m) of $^{1}/_{4}$-inch (6mm)-wide grosgrain ribbon in red

1$^{1}/_{8}$ yds (1m) of $^{5}/_{8}$-inch (1.5cm)-wide grosgrain ribbon in red

Special note: 1$^{3}/_{4}$-inch (4.5cm)-wide bias is used on several items in the nursery suite. For ease of construction, make a total of 14 yds (12.8m) of bias to be used on valances, curtains, and 12 x 16-inch (30 x 41cm) pillow.

Crib Bumper

MATERIALS

7 yds (6.5m) of $\frac{7}{8}$-inch (2cm)-wide grosgrain ribbon in red

7 yds (6.5m) of $\frac{5}{8}$-inch (1.5cm)-wide single-face satin ribbon in yellow gold

7 yds (6.5m) of $\frac{3}{8}$-inch (1cm)-wide grosgrain ribbon in Capri blue

7 yds (6.5m) of $\frac{1}{4}$-inch (6mm)-wide single-face satin ribbon in forest

5 yds (4.5m) of $1\frac{1}{2}$-inch (4cm)-wide satin ribbon pattern "Toybox" by Gear®

$\frac{7}{8}$ yd (80cm) of 54-inch (1.4m)-wide denim fabric

$1\frac{1}{2}$ yds (1.5m) of 45-inch (1.2m)-wide red polka-dot fabric

$1\frac{1}{4}$ yd (1.25m) (minimum) of 45-inch (1.2m)-wide cotton plaid (extra may be needed to match plaids)

1 pkg bumper batting, 10 inches wide by 15 feet long (25.5cm x 4.5m)

Simplicity Pattern #7674 or other commercial pattern

Thread to match

DIRECTIONS

Note: Use $\frac{1}{2}$-inch (1.5cm) seams throughout. Sew all fabrics right side together.

1. Cut denim into four pieces, each one $7\frac{1}{2}$ x 45 inches (19cm x 1.2m). Cut red polka-dot fabric into four pieces, each one $4\frac{1}{2}$ x 45 inches (11.5cm x 1.2m). Stitch denim together end to end to make one long piece $7\frac{1}{2}$ x 180 inches (19cm x 4.5m). Repeat for polka-dot fabric.

2. Sew polka-dot fabric to denim along 180-inch (4.5m) length. Press seam open.

3. Center "Toybox" ribbon over seam. Topstitch in place.

4. Cut plaid fabric into four pieces, each one 11 x 45 inches (28cm x 1.2m). Stitch together, matching plaids as needed.

5. Cut solid-color ribbons into 18-inch (50cm) lengths. Match together one ribbon of each color, creating fourteen sets of four ribbons each. Attach these to bumper according to markings on Simplicity pattern. *Note:* Bumper will be longer than pattern by width of headboard. Adjust ties accordingly.

6. Construct and finish bumper according to Simplicity pattern directions.

Dust Ruffles

MATERIALS for
Short Dust Ruffle

12⅛ yds (11.5m) of ¼-inch (6mm)-wide single-face satin ribbon in yellow gold

12⅛ yd (11.5m) of ⅜-inch (1cm)-wide grosgrain ribbon in red

9⅜ yd (8.8m) of ⅞-inch (2cm)-wide satin ribbon pattern "Crayola® Color Fun"

Simplicity Pattern #7674 or other commercial pattern

54-inch (1.4m)-wide denim fabric as required

MATERIALS for
Long Dust Ruffle

Simplicity Pattern #7674 or other commercial pattern

45-inch (1.2m)-wide plaid cotton, double the amount stated on the pattern envelope, allowing extra for matching plaids; long dust ruffle depth is increased to 20 inches (51cm) from 10 inches (25.5cm) on short dust ruffle

DIRECTIONS

1. For short dust ruffle, cut out denim according to pattern pieces. Construct according to pattern directions. Hem as instructed.

2. Topstitch ⅜-inch red grosgrain ribbon, 1 inch (2.5cm) from finished hem on all sides. Next, sew ⅞-inch "Crayola" ribbon, ¾ inch (2cm) from red ribbon. Finish by sewing ¼-inch yellow gold satin ribbon ½ inch (1.5cm) from "Crayola" ribbon.

3. From remaining red grosgrain ribbon and yellow satin ribbon, cut each color into eight equal lengths. Tie each piece into a small bow. Attach red bow randomly to red ribbon on dust ruffle. Repeat for yellow bows.

4. For long dust ruffle, use Simplicity pattern pieces and increase depth of ruffle to 20 inches (51cm) plus hem (or correct length for desired crib). Match plaids as needed. Assemble following Simplicity pattern instructions.

5. Layer short dust ruffle on top of long dust ruffle for the finished look.

Quilt

MATERIALS

2½ yds (2.5m) of 1½-inch (4cm)-wide satin ribbon pattern "Toybox" by Gear®

½ yd (50cm) of ⅞-inch (2cm)-wide grosgrain ribbon in red

½ yd (50cm) of ⅜-inch (1cm)-wide grosgrain ribbon in red

⅙ yd (15cm) of 45-inch (1.2m)-wide red polka-dot fabric

2 yds (2m) of 45-inch (1.2m)-wide navy striped fabric

½ yd (50cm) of 54-inch (1.4m)-wide denim fabric

Simplicity Pattern #7674 or other commercial pattern

45-inch (1.2m)-wide cotton plaid per pattern requirements

Quilt batting

Fusible web

Threads to match

Water soluble pen

Ruler

Cotton fabric pieces for applique center panel:

Muslin (background) 16½ x 19 inches (42 x 48cm)

Yellow gold (floor) 16½ x 7 inches (42 x 17.5cm)

Red (block) 4½ x 4½ inches (11.5 x 11.5cm)

Medium blue (teddy's clothes) 9 x 10 inches (23 x 25.5cm)

Navy blue (shoes, faces, fishing line) 8 x 10 inches (20 x 25.5cm)
White (collar and cuffs) 5 x 8 inches (13 x 20cm)

Yellow (fish) 2½ x 3 inches (6.5 x 7.5cm)

Green (fish) 5 x 5½ inches (13 x 14cm)

Brown (teddy face and paws) 6 x 9 inches (15 x 23cm)

DIRECTIONS

Note: Use 1/4-inch (6mm) seams throughout pieced areas. Use 1/2-inch (1.5cm) seams everywhere else.

1. To make center applique panel, sew muslin to yellow along 16 1/2-inch (42cm) side to make background. Press seams to gold. Set aside.

2. From navy fabric, cut a piece 8 x 4 1/2 inches (20 x 11.5cm). Set remainder aside.

3. Following manufacturer's directions, fuse all applique fabrics to fusible web, including 8 x 4 1/2-inch navy piece.

4. Trace applique pattern pieces onto appropriate fabrics and cut out.

5. Using quilt photograph on page 94 as a guide, fuse applique pieces in place on background panel.

6. From remaining navy blue fabric, cut 1 1/4-inch (3cm)-wide bias strips, piecing as needed to make 25 inches (63.5cm) of finished bias. Fold bias in half lengthwise and sew together using a 1/4-inch (6mm) seam. Press seam to center back to conceal raw edges.

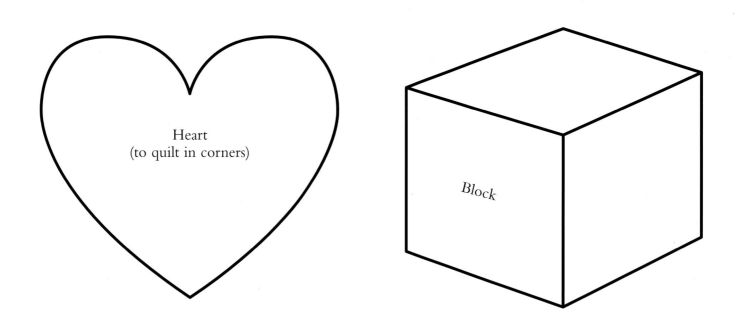

Heart
(to quilt in corners)

Block

Enlarge pattern pieces by 25 percent

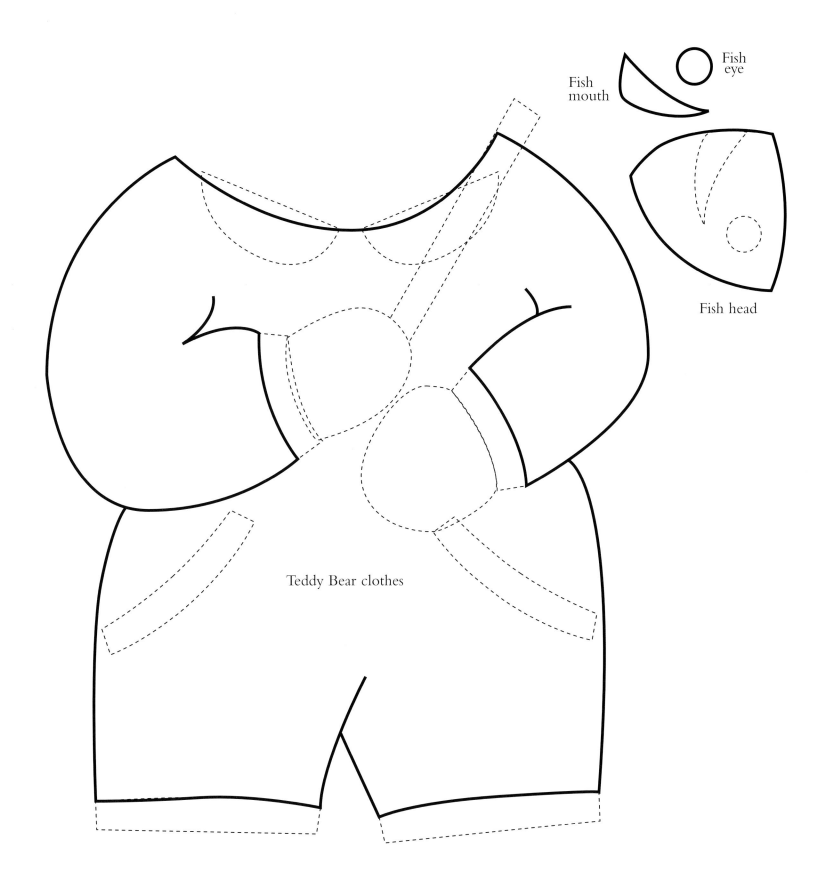

Fish mouth

Fish eye

Fish head

Teddy Bear clothes

Enlarge pattern pieces by 25 percent

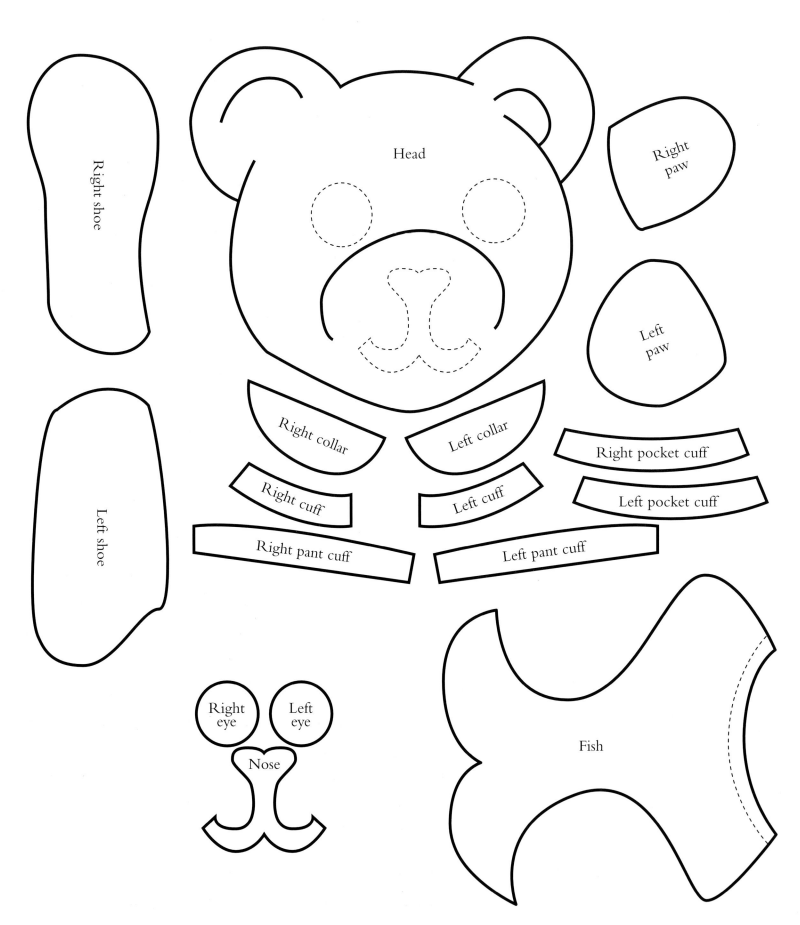

Right shoe

Head

Right paw

Left paw

Left shoe

Right collar

Left collar

Right pocket cuff

Right cuff

Left cuff

Left pocket cuff

Right pant cuff

Left pant cuff

Right eye

Left eye

Nose

Fish

Enlarge pattern pieces by 25 percent

7. Use ⅜-inch red grosgrain ribbon for fishing pole. Topstitch in place.

8. With bias, create a meandering fishline. Topstitch in place.

9. Satin stitch over all raw edges of the fused shapes in the appliqued panel.

10. With water-soluble pen, mark all quilting lines on background of center panel. Set aside.

11. From striped fabric, cutting lengthwise with the stripe, cut two pieces each 6 x 26½ inches (15 x 67.5cm) and two pieces each 6 x 16½ inches (15 x 42cm). Sew "Toybox" ribbon to each piece of stripe 2 inches (5cm) from outside edge.

12. From red polka-dot fabric, cut four 6 x 6-inch (15 x 15cm) squares. Sew one square to each end of the 26½ x 6-inch pieces.

13. Sew 16½ x 6-inch panels to each end of center applique panel.

14. Sew striped units to each side of center panel, matching corners cleanly.

15. From denim, cut two pieces each 4 x 27 inches (10 x 68.5cm) and two pieces each 4 x 44 inches (10cm x 1.2m). Sew short pieces to top and bottom of center panel. Sew long pieces to each side, to finish quilt top.

16. Place quilt top on batting and topstitch around outside edge to hold.

17. Assemble ruffle from plaid cotton as instructed in Simplicity pattern.

18. Pin finished ruffle to right side of quilt top, following the Simplicity pattern directions for the wallhanging. Substitute ruffle for piping in the directions.

19. Cut quilt backing from remaining striped fabric using the Simplicity pattern piece.

20. Assemble quilt according to directions for the wallhanging.

21. Following the Simplicity pattern directions, baste layers of quilt together to hold.

22. Complete machine quilting as follows:
    - outline quilt ⅛ inch (3mm) from all applique pieces on center panel
    - quilt along all marked lines in center panel
    - quilt straight lines between stripes on striped fabric
    - quilt a heart in each corner using heart template
    - quilt a hand-drawn serpentine line in denim border meeting at each corner

23. From ⅞-inch red grosgrain ribbon, tie a bow and attach to bear at collar.

Curtains

Size: 38 inches wide by 44 inches long (1 X 1.2m)

MATERIALS for four panels

6 yds (5.5m) of 45-inch (1.2m)-wide cotton plaid (allow extra to match plaids)

¼ yd (23cm) of 54-inch (1.4m)-wide denim

2¼ yds (2m) of 45-inch (1.2m)-wide red polka-dot fabric

½ yd (50cm) of 45-inch (1.2m)-wide navy striped fabric

4 yds (4m) of 45-inch (1.2m)-wide muslin

Thread

DIRECTIONS

Note: Use ¼-inch (6mm) seams throughout. Sew all fabrics right sides together. Make curtains in pairs with a right and left panel in each pair

1. From denim, cut four 6 x 6-inch (15 x 15cm) squares. From plaid, matching as needed, cut four 33-inch (84cm)-wide x 41-inch (1m)-long panels. From red polka-dot fabric, refer to cutting layout and cut out four 33 x 5-inch (84 x 13cm) and four 41 x 5-inch (1m x 13cm) pieces for front of curtain panels. Set remainder aside. From navy striped fabric, cut 1¾-inch (4.5cm)-wide diagonal strips, piecing as needed for a finished length of 320 inches (8.2m).

2. For one curtain panel, stitch one 33-inch (84cm) bias to one 33-inch (84cm) red polka-dot panel. Stitch one 41-inch (1m) bias to one 41-inch (1m) red polka dot panel. Press all seams to navy. Sew 6 x 6-inch (15 x 15cm) denim square to end of pieced 41-inch (1m) panel. Stitch 33-inch (84cm) pieced panel to 33-inch (84cm) edge of plaid panel. Stitch denim pieced panel to plaid panel, aligning denim square with pieced fabric on plaid panel. Repeat. Then, make two more panels with the denim on the opposite side.

3. To make lining, cut four panels of muslin 33 x 41 inches (84cm x 1m), four panels of red polka-dot fabric 33 x 6½-inch (84 x 16.5cm), and four panels of red polka-dot fabric 47 x 6½ inches (1.2m x16.5cm). Stitch 33 x 6½-inch panel to lower edge of muslin. Stitch 47 x 6½-inch panel to left side of muslin. Press.

4. Pin curtain panel and lining together with red sides matching. Stitch around all four sides, leaving a 5-inch (13cm) opening on the plaid side for turning. Clip corners and turn. Press seams flat. Slip-stitch the opening closed.

5. For casing at top of curtain, topstitch 1 inch down from top edge. Stitch second row of stitching 1⅛-inches (2.6cm) from first row across entire curtain panel. With seam ripper, open seam between rows of casing stitches. Repeat for remaining panels, making two left facing panels and two right facing panels.

Reversible Curtain Tiebacks

MATERIALS

3⅛ yd (3.1m) of ⅞-inch (2cm)-
wide ribbon pattern "Trains" by
Gear®, cut into four lengths

½ yd (50cm) of 45-inch (1.2m)
navy striped fabric

⅜ yd (34.5cm) of 54-inch (1.4m)-
wide denim

Eight ½-inch (1.5cm) bone rings

Sewing needle and thread

DIRECTIONS

Note: Use ¼-inch (6mm) seams throughout. Sew all fabrics right sides together.

1. From denim, cut four fabric pieces 5 x 14 inches (13 x 35.5cm). From striped fabric, cut four pieces 5 x 14 inches (13 x 35.5cm), cutting lengthwise with stripe (see illustration below).

2. Sew one denim piece to one striped piece along 5-inch (13cm) side, creating one piece 5 x 28 inches (13 x 70cm). Repeat with remaining pieces. Press seams open.

3. Fold tieback in half lengthwise and stitch. Turn to right side. Press with seam placed at center back. Repeat for each tieback.

4. Fold raw edges inside ½ inch (1.5cm) at each end. Press to hold.

5. Center "Trains" ribbon over tieback. Fold under ends of ribbon into center of tieback. Topstitch in place. Sew two pairs of tiebacks with ribbon alternating so "Trains" are always right side up.

6. Sew one bone ring to wrong side of tieback at each end for easy hanging.

one pair

denim   stripe

stripe   denim

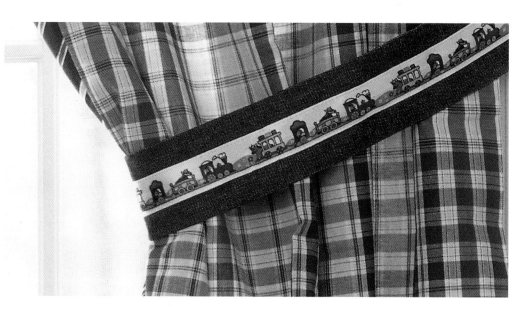

Valances

Size: 40 inches (100cm) wide by 12 inches (30cm) high χ 4 inches (10cm) deep

MATERIALS for

two valances

1²/₃ yd (1.6m) of 1¹/₂-inch (4cm)-wide ribbon pattern "Toybox" by Gear®

1²/₃ yd (1.6m) of ⁷/₈-inch (2cm)-wide ribbon pattern "Crayola® Color Fun"

1 yd (1m) of 54-inch (1.4)-wide denim

¹/₄ yd (23cm) of 45-inch (1.2m)-wide red polka-dot fabric

¹/₄ yd (23cm) of 45-inch (1.2m)-wide navy striped fabric

Quilt batting, four pieces 54 x 18 inches (1.4m x 50cm)

¹/₄-inch (6mm) foamcore board 40 x 60 inches (1 x 1.5m)

Sharp utility knife with a fresh blade

T-square ruler and/or metal ruler

Hot glue gun and glue sticks

Thread

DIRECTIONS

Note: Use ¹/₄-inch (6mm) seams throughout.

1. From foamcore, cut two pieces 49 inches (1.3 m) long x 12 inches (30cm) wide.

2. Measure in 4¹/₂ inches (11.5cm) from each end. Mark lightly from top to bottom on wrong side of foamcore. With utility knife, score along marking, being careful *not* to cut all the way through foamcore. Gently trim a "V" shape with utility knife along scored mark. Carefully bend foamcore to make a right-angle corner. Fold to inside of "V" cut and release. Do this to both pieces of foamcore. Set aside.

3. From scraps of foamcore, cut four 4 x 4-inch (10 x 10cm) squares. Cut each square in half diagonally. Glue one half to the other to reinforce triangle brace. Repeat to make four. Set aside.

4. Cut four 1¹/₂ x 1¹/₂-inch (4 x 4cm) squares from foamcore. Repeat process for large triangle braces. Make four. Set aside.

5. For valance cover: Cut two denim pieces 17 x 24 inches (43 x 61cm). Cut one red polka-dot fabric piece 17 x 7 inches (43 x 17.5cm). From navy striped fabric, cut two 17-inch (43cm) lengths of 1³/₄-inch bias.

6. Stitch 1¹/₂-inch "Toybox" ribbon 4¹/₂ inches (11.5cm) from lower edge of denim piece. Stitch ⁷/₈-inch "Crayola" ribbon 1 inch (2.5cm) above "Toybox" ribbon. Repeat.

7. To complete valance cover: Stitch bias strip to each side of red polka-dot fabric. Press. Stitch denim to each side of bias strip. Press seams.

8. To assemble valance: Mark center back of foamcore. Next, place valance cover right side down on work surface. Place two layers of quilt batting on top.

9. Center foamcore on top of fabric and batting. Glue fabric to back side of foamcore valance using hot glue gun. Start at center top, then glue center bottom. Work outward from center, pulling fabric firmly to keep it taut on the front side of valance. Clip fabric at notched "V" cuts on foamcore to ease fabric. Trim excess fabric from corners before gluing.

10. Fold valance at "V"-cut notch. Glue 4-inch (10cm) foamcore triangle brace at top of corner 1¼ inches (3cm) down from top edge. Place one in each top corner. Hold brace in place until glue is *completely* set. Repeat for other corner. Glue small braces in each bottom corner placing them 2 inches (5cm) from bottom edge.

11. Once glue is completely set, hot glue along all edges where brace meets valance to reinforce the brace.

12. Valance is designed to rest on top of curtain rod without additional installation. If more stability is required, tack valance at sides to wall or window frame with small brads.

PLAY IT SAFE

Following is a list of ideas that will help you make your home a safter place for the baby. Check the reading list in the back of the book for additional sources of information on fully baby-proofing your home.

⋆ Assemble a first-aid kit for babies

⋆ Install carbon monoxide detectors and smoke detectors, and have fire extinguishers on hand

⋆ Be sure crib slats are no more than $2^3/8$ inches (6cm) apart—if a soda can fits through the slats, they are probably too wide

⋆ Have a safe, secure changing table, complete with a strap

⋆ Make sure rear-facing infant car seat is properly installed

⋆ Bolt furniture such as bookcases to wall

⋆ Use retractable cords on window shades and telephones

⋆ Apply foam edges to sharp corners

⋆ Install baby gates at tops and bottoms of stairs

⋆ Use drawer and cabinet latches, especially in kitchen and bathroom, where sharp objects and medications may be kept

⋆ Plug electrical outlets

Look at your home through your baby's eyes. Get down on your hands and knees and crawl around to discover potential trouble!

Lamp Shade

MATERIALS

Purchased lamp with lamp shade

$1/3$ yd (30.5cm) of 45-inch (1.2m)-wide cotton plaid

$1/4$ yd (23cm) of 45-inch (1.2m)-wide navy striped fabric

$1^{1}/4$ yd (1.25m) of $7/8$-inch (2cm)-wide satin ribbon pattern "Trains" by Gear®

$1^{1}/8$ yds (1.1m) of $5/8$-inch (1.5cm)-wide grosgrain ribbon in red

Thread to match

Optional: Hot glue gun and glue sticks

DIRECTIONS

Note: Use $1/4$-inch (6mm) seams throughout. Sew all fabric right sides together.

1. To prepare bias strip, cut $4^{1}/2$-inch (11.5cm)-wide diagonal strips from navy striped fabric. Piece together as needed to make a strip $4^{1}/2$ inches (11.5cm) wide x 45 inches (1.2m) long.

2. Sew bias strip to lower edge of plaid. Press seams toward strip.

3. Topstitch $7/8$-inch "Trains" ribbon to bias strip $1/2$ inch (1.5cm) from seam.

4. Sew side seams together, aligning plaids, seams, and ribbon. Press seam open.

5. Turn under $1/4$ inch (6mm) on raw edge of bias strip. Press. Fold strip in half. Align fold with seam and topstitch in place to enclose all raw edges.

6. To make casing: At top of lamp shade cover, fold under $1/4$ inch (6mm) hem. Press. Measure 2 inches (5cm) from fold and fold again. Stitch along edge of $1/4$-inch (6mm) hem. To complete casing, stitch again $5/8$ inch (1.5cm) from first stitching.

7. Fold lamp shade cover in half, using seam as center back and fold as center front. Mark center front with a pin. Carefully cut a $1/2$-inch (1.5cm) vertical slit on each side of center front.

8. Thread $5/8$-inch-wide grosgrain through casing. Place cover on shade. Gather cover to fit top of shade. Adjust gathers evenly. Tie ribbon in a bow to secure gathers.

Optional: Hot glue cover to shade to hold in place permanently.

Wastebasket

MATERIALS

2½ yds (2.5m) of ¼-inch (6mm)-wide grosgrain ribbon in red

⅞ yd (80cm) of ⅞-inch (2cm)-wide satin ribbon pattern "Crayola® Color Fun"

⅞ yd (80cm) of 1½-inch (4cm)-wide satin ribbon pattern "Toybox" by Gear®

2 yds (2m) of ⅞-inch (2cm)-wide grosgrain ribbon in red, cut into eight 9-inch (23cm) lengths

2 yds (2m) of ⅞-inch (2cm)-wide grosgrain ribbon in Capri blue, cut into eight 9-inch (23cm) lengths

Wastebasket in yellow

Hot glue gun and glue sticks

DIRECTIONS

1. Measure down 4 inches (10cm) from top rim of wastebasket. Mark lightly with a pencil around entire wastebasket.

2. Alternating red and blue ⅞-inch ribbons, space evenly around basket: Place raw edge of ribbon ⅛ inch (3mm) above mark and glue in place. Stretch ribbon to bottom of wastebasket and glue in place. Repeat, using all sixteen ribbon lengths.

3. Next, glue ⅜-inch-wide red grosgrain ribbon over raw edges. Align ribbon with pencil marking. Fold under raw edges at end and glue in place.

4. Glue ribbons around top rim of wastebasket, aligning the 1½-inch-wide "Toybox" ribbon directly above the red grosgrain ribbon already in place; follow with ⅜-inch red ribbon, then ⅞-inch "Crayola" ribbon. Leave a ¼-inch (6mm) space and finish with ⅜-inch red ribbon.

Gift Box Pillow

MATERIALS

4½ yds (4.5m) of ⅞-inch (2cm)-wide grosgrain ribbon in red

½ yd (50cm) of 45-inch (1.2m)-wide navy striped fabric

24 oz pkg of polyester fiberfill

Thread

Optional: Hot glue gun and glue stick

DIRECTIONS

Note: Use ¼-inch (6mm) seams throughout. Sew with right sides together.

1. Cut six 9 x 9-inch (23 x 23 cm) squares from navy striped fabric.

2. Stitch one 9-inch square to another 9-inch square along one side. Repeat until four squares are joined together. Pin one 9-inch square to tops of "box," clipping at corners. Stitch. Repeat for bottom of "box," leaving a 4-inch (10cm) opening

3. Turn to right side and stuff firmly, keeping box shape. Pay special attention to corners. Slip-stitch closed.

4. From ribbon, cut two 33-inch (84cm) lengths. Starting at top of box, wrap ribbon around to meet on other side of box. Secure. Repeat in other direction with remaining length of ribbon.

5. From remaining ribbon, cut a 15-inch (38cm) length and set it aside. Following General Bow Techniques on page 140, make a gift bow with ten loops from remaining ribbon. Tie loops securely with the 15-inch length of ribbon. Attach to top of box, covering ribbon raw edges. Secure.

Square Pillow

MATERIALS

3/8 yd (34.5cm) of 7/8-inch (2cm)-wide ribbon pattern "Trains" by Gear®

3/8 yd (34.5cm) of 5/8-inch (1.5cm)-wide satin ribbon in yellow gold

3/8 yd (34.5cm) of 7/8-inch (2cm)-wide satin ribbon pattern "Crayola® Color Fun"

3/8 yd (34.5cm) of 1 1/2-inch (4cm)-wide satin ribbon pattern "Toybox" by Gear®

Simplicity Pattern 7674

54-inch (1.4m)-wide denim, amount as required by Simplicity pattern

45-inch (1.2m)-wide red polka-dot fabric, amount as required by Simplicity pattern

45-inch (1.2m)-wide navy striped fabric, amount as required by Simplicity pattern

12-inch (30cm) square pillow form

Thread

DIRECTIONS

1. Following Simplicity pattern instructions, cut center panel piece from denim. Cut end pieces from navy striped fabric. Cut ruffle and back of pillow from red polka-dot fabric. Cut an additional strip of red polka-dot fabric measuring 2 x 13 inches (5 x 33cm).

2. Stitch striped pieces to top and bottom of center denim piece as instructed. Press seams open.

3. Starting at bottom of the pillow and working to top, stitch 1 1/2-inch "Toybox" ribbon 3/4 inch (2cm) from striped fabric. Next, turn under 1/4-inch (6mm) on each side of 2 x 13-inch red fabric strip, then stitch 3/4 inch (2cm) from "Toybox" ribbon. Stitch 7/8-inch "Crayola" ribbon 5/8 inch (1.5cm) from red polka-dot fabric. Stitch 5/8-inch-wide yellow ribbon 5/8 inch (1.5cm) from "Crayola" ribbon. Finally, stitch 7/8-inch "Trains" ribbon 5/8 inch (1.5cm) from yellow ribbon.

4. Finish pillow according to Simplicity pattern directions.

Chapter Four

PLAYFUL OUTFITS, ACCESSORIES & TOYS

DRESSING THE LITTLE ONE AND organizing his or her many things is one of the challenges that comes with having a new baby. Tiny hair clips add a pretty touch to any little girl's wardrobe, and the ones shown here can be made in just a few minutes. For a lively look, go "wild" with the infant overalls trimmed with Offray's premade ribbon animals. These are easily stitched to purchased garments for a one-of-a-kind look. Add cute animal caps to complete the ensembles.

Storage is certainly important for the many toys the new baby will receive. I've used chenille fabrics in coordinating patterns, adorned with ribbons and premade ribbon roses, to create this unique toy box. Another simple and useful item is the dishtowel organizer, designed to hang on the wall above the changing table. Made from two dishtowels and accented with ribbons, it is perfect for keeping baby powder, lotions, and other small items close at hand.

Finally, a selection of red, black, and white toys and accessories stimulates the baby's vision with sharp contrasts of color. A set of soft blocks, a mobile, a crib toy, and a matching picture frame makes a darling gift or a fun project for the new mom.

Towel Pocket Organizer ∼∽∼∽∼

Keep necessary changing items close at hand with this attractive organizer made from two dishtowels and edged with ribbon.

MATERIALS

$4\frac{1}{3}$ yds (4m) of $\frac{5}{8}$-inch (1.5cm)-wide satin ribbon in white

$1\frac{2}{3}$ yds (1.6m) of $\frac{5}{8}$-inch (1.5cm)-wide satin ribbon in blue

$1\frac{2}{3}$ yds (1.6m) of $\frac{3}{8}$-inch (1cm)-wide satin ribbon in light green

$1\frac{2}{3}$ yds (1.6m) of $\frac{5}{8}$-inch (1.5cm)-wide novelty printed satin ribbon

3 premade ribbon roses

Two 18 x 28-inch (50 x 70cm) terry kitchen towels in coordinating colors (We used a solid blue towel and a blue and white check towel)

One $\frac{5}{8}$-inch (1.5cm) wooden dowel, 24 inches (61cm) long

White paint

Thread

DIRECTIONS

1. Stitch a length of $\frac{3}{8}$-inch light green ribbon, $\frac{5}{8}$-inch printed ribbon, and $\frac{5}{8}$-inch white ribbon to the top and bottom edges of the blue towel. Raw edges of all ribbons are turned to the back of the towel before stitching. Refer to photograph for placement.

2. Stitch a length of $\frac{5}{8}$-inch white ribbon along each side of the towel, approximately $\frac{5}{8}$ inch (1.5cm) from the edge. Bottom raw edge is turned to the back of the towel. Extend top edge of ribbon 3 inches (7.5cm) to allow for loop. Turn top of ribbon lengths back to create loops. Hand baste with a few stitches to hold.

3. Cut two 4-inch (10cm) lengths of $\frac{5}{8}$-inch white ribbon for remaining loops. Evenly space loops and hand-baste to top of towel. Insert dowel through loops and make any adjustments so that the towel hangs evenly. Machine-stitch loops to towel to secure.

4. Following General bow Techniques on page 140, make four small two-loop bows from 12-inch (30cm) lengths of $\frac{5}{8}$-inch white ribbon. Hand-stitch each bow to the base of each loop.

5. For pockets: Cut three 6 x 5 inch (15 x 13cm) rectangles and three 8 x 5 inch (20 x 13cm) rectangles from blue and white check towel. Note that pockets are all 5 inches (13cm) deep. Cut pockets so top edge is along the finished side edge of the towel. This will eliminate the need to hem the top edge of each pocket.

6. On the three large pockets, stitch a length of $\frac{3}{8}$-inch light green ribbon, $\frac{5}{8}$-inch printed ribbon, and $\frac{5}{8}$-inch blue ribbon. Follow photograph for placement.

7. On the three small pockets, stitch a length of ⅝-inch blue satin ribbon. Cut three 12-inch (30cm) lengths of the blue ribbon. Following General Bow Techniques on page 140, form each into a two-loop bow. Stitch bows to center of each pocket. Stitch a ribbon rose to the center of each bow.

8. On all pockets, turn back side and bottom raw edges ½ inch (1.5cm) and baste to hold.

9. Alternating small and large pockets, pin pockets to blue towel. Machine stitch along the sides and bottom of each pocket.

10. Paint dowel white. Insert dowel through ribbon loops.

Ribbon and Chenille Toy Box

A softly padded chenille box adds charm to baby's room and keeps all the little toys in one place. Dress up your little one's room and make use of any extra chenille by sewing these charming stuffed animals. Use Simplicity Pattern 8418—for the rabbit improvise extra-long ears!

MATERIALS for a box measuring **11 x 11 x 19 inches (28 x 28 x 48cm)**

7/8-inch (2cm)-wide grosgrain ribbon in two colors

Assorted premade ribbon roses

Chenille fabric (craft cuts used here)

Small unpainted wooden toy box

1/4-inch (6mm) foamcore: two pieces cut to 9 x 17 inches (23 x 43cm) and two pieces cut to 9 x 9 inches (23 x 23cm)

Quilt batting

White spray paint

Glue gun and glue sticks

DIRECTIONS

1. Spray-paint the interior, back, and outside edges of box.

2. Cut foamcore to fit top, front, and sides of box, minus 1 inch (2.5cm) all around.

3. Cut quilt batting to size of foamcore shapes. Glue to one side of foamcore.

4. Cut chenille fabric to size of foamcore plus 3 inches (7.5cm) around. Wrap over batting side of foamcore and bring raw edges to wrong side. Glue, tape, or staple to back.

5. Glue grosgrain ribbon to outside edges of box top, front, and side. Miter corners.

6. Glue chenille panels to box top, front, and sides.

7. Following General Bow Techniques on page 140, make four bows from lengths of grosgrain ribbon. Glue to each corner of top.

8. Hot glue premade ribbon roses to corners of box front and center top. Make sure roses are glued securely and check them periodically.

Baby Overalls

Wild animals made of ribbons trim purchased overalls, creating one-of-a-kind outfits for baby boy or girl. Be certain to stitch the ribbons and animals securely to the clothing and check them before each wearing—babies love to put things in their mouths, and any small loose items within baby's reach present a choking hazard.

Girl's Ribbon Jungle Outfit

MATERIALS

1 yd (1m) (approximately)★ of pink ribbon flower garland

3/8 yd (34.5cm) of 3/8-inch (1cm) apple green grosgrain ribbon

1/8 yd (11.5cm) of 3/8-inch (1cm) emerald green grosgrain ribbon

1/3 yd (30cm) of 5/8-inch (1.5cm) emerald green grosgrain ribbon

1/8 yd (11.5cm) of 3/8-inch (1cm) pink satin ribbon

1 pkg premade Allie ribbon elephant

1 pkg premade Tina and Tiny small ribbon elephants

1 pkg premade Milo and Missy small ribbon monkeys

Infant-size overalls and shirt

★*Note:* Measure neckline of overalls to determine the exact amount of garland needed to sew around the edge. Add 9 inches (23cm) to this measurement for extra flowers that will be cut from garland and sewn to overalls.

DIRECTIONS

Note: Overalls must have snap crotch.

1. Hand-stitch ribbon garland around neckline of overalls.

2. To create ruffled ribbon leaves at bottom of left pant leg, cut 5/8-inch green grosgrain ribbon into two 6-inch (15cm) lengths. Cut one end of each ribbon into a sharp "V." Fold back the other end 1/2 inch (1.5cm) from raw edge. Beginning at folded end, machine-stitch with long gathering stitches down center of ribbon. Pull stitches slightly to gather.

3. Open up pant leg. Pin leaves to overall legs and machine-stitch in place, stitching on top of gathering stitches.

4. To create folded leaves, cut 3/8-inch green grosgrain ribbons into 4 1/2-inch (11.5cm) lengths. Cut ends on the diagonal. Fold slightly off-center. Pin and hand-stitch two apple green folded leaves on left pant leg, one on each side of the ruffled leaves. Pin and hand-stitch one emerald green and one apple green folded leaf to the right bodice of the overalls.

5. Hand-stitch large ribbon elephant amongst the leaves on the left pant leg.

6. Hand-stitch the small ribbon elephant and monkey amongst the leaves on the bodice.

7. Clip ribbon flowers from remaining garland. Hand-stitch flowers among the leaves and animals.

8. Make a small two-loop bow with the pink satin ribbon. Stitch a ribbon flower to the center of the bow.

9. Stitch completed bow to center neckline of shirt.

Boy's Ribbon Jungle Overalls

MATERIALS

1 yd (1m) of ⅝-inch (1.5cm)-wide grosgrain ribbon in apple green

⅝ yd (1.5m) of ⅝-inch (1.5cm)-wide grosgrain ribbon in green

½ yd (50cm) of ⅜-inch (1cm)-wide grosgrain ribbon in apple green

⅓ yd (30.5cm) of ⅜-inch (1cm)-wide grosgrain ribbon in emerald

1 pkg premade Libby ribbon lion

1 pkg premade Leo ribbon lion

1 pkg premade Liam and Lucy small ribbon lions

1 pkg premade Gerry ribbon giraffe

1 pkg premade Gus and Gobby small ribbon giraffes

1 pkg premade Zippy ribbon zebra

1 pkg premade Zoie and Zack small ribbon zebras

Infant-size denim overalls and red shirt

DIRECTIONS

Note: Overalls must have snap crotch so that single layer of pant legs can be machine-stitched to ribbon leaves.

1. Using ½-inch-wide ribbons, follow General Flower Techniques for Ruffled Leaves on page 139 to create ruffled ribbon leaves at bottom of pants legs. Cut ribbons as specified: For right leg, cut one apple green leaf 8 inches (20cm) long, one bright green leaf 5 inches (12.5 cm) long, one green leaf 9 inches (23cm) long, and one green leaf 4 inches (10cm) long. For left leg, cut one bright green leaf 9 inches (23cm) long, one bright green leaf 6 inches (15cm) long, one bright green leaf 5 inches (12.5cm) long, and one green leaf 7 inches (17.5cm) long.

2. Hand-stitch Gerry and Gus giraffes and Leo lion securely to right leg.

Hand-stitch Libby and Liam lions and Zippy zebra to left leg.

3. Following General Flower Techniques for Folded Leaves on page 139, make folded leaves as follows: Attach two bright green folded leaves and one green folded leaf to top pocket, one bright green and one green folded leaf to left side pocket, one bright green and one green folded leaf to back right pocket, and one green folded leaf to upper right sleeve of shirt.

4. Hand-stitch remaining ribbon animals among the folded leaves.

Hats for Baby

*K*eep sun off the little one's head with one of these adorable hats trimmed with premade ribbon animals.

"Take Me to the Zoo" Hat

MATERIALS

1 pkg Bobo and Buffy premade ribbon bears

1 pkg Gus and Gobby premade ribbon giraffe

1 pkg Liam and Lucy premade ribbon lions

1 pkg Zoie and Zack premade ribbon zebra

1 infant-size baseball-style hat

White felt remnant

Black and brown embroidery floss

$^5/_8$-inch (1.5cm) brown button

Iron-on transfer pen

Threads

DIRECTIONS

1. Trace the hat brim pattern on page 124 on paper. Trim $^1/_4$ inch (6mm) from the paper brim and use as a pattern. Cut out the felt.

2. Use transfer pen to trace the backwards letters from the pattern on page 124. Follow the instructions to iron the letters to the felt. When they are transferred, they will be readable.

3. Use two strands of embroidery floss to embroider the letters.

4. Use all six strands to outline the edges of felt with a buttonhole stitch. Also embroider the lower edge of the cap, except the elasticized area.

5. Stitch the brown button to the top of the cap. Glue the felt to the brim and stitch all the ribbon animals securely around the edge of the cap front.

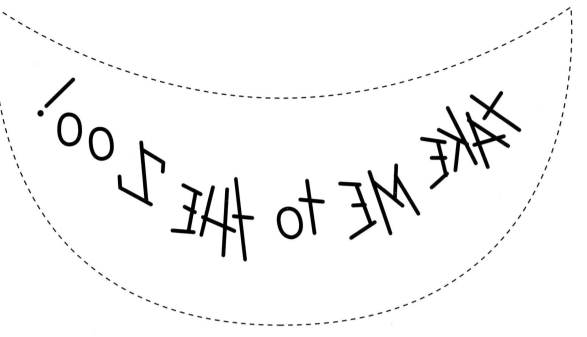

"I Love Monkeys" Hat

MATERIALS

1 pkg Molly premade ribbon monkey

1 pkg Milo and Missy premade ribbon monkeys

1/4 yd (23cm) of 1/4-inch (6mm)-wide double-face satin ribbon in mauve

Purple felt remnant, 7 inches (18cm) square

1 hot pink hat

Embroidery floss in magenta

Glue

Thread

DIRECTIONS

1. Cut out one felt heart and use the embroidery floss to embellish the edge with a buttonhole stitch.

2. Stitch the heart to the hat so the pointed part is on the brim.

3. Stitch the three monkeys to the hat as shown in the photograph.

4. Make a simple bow from ribbon and trim tails on an angle. Stitch to hat as shown.

"I Love Peanut Butter" Hat

MATERIALS

4 premade ribbon swirl roses in white

1 pkg Allie premade ribbon elephants

1 hat

White fabric paint

Thread

DIRECTIONS

1. After practicing, carefully paint the words "i love peanut butter ...Mmm" as pictured on the hat below onto the edge of the hat. Let dry!

2. Stitch the elephant and roses in place, as shown in the photograph.

Baby Hair Clips

*T*hese sweet little clips are so easy to make that you can create one to go with every outfit.

MATERIALS

⅛ yd (11.5cm) of ⅜-inch (1cm) ribbon in a variety of colors and designs

Variety of premade ribbon flowers and/or bows

Purchased small baby hairclips

Thread

Glue gun and glue sticks

DIRECTIONS

1. Stitch an assortment of ribbon flowers to short lengths of ribbon.

2. Using photograph as a guide, glue lengths of ribbon to hair clips, covering both sides when necessary.

A babe in a house is a well-spring of pleasure, a messenger of peace and love, a resting-place for innocence on earth; a link between angels and men.

—M.F. TUPPER

Baby's First Toys

What's black and white and red all over? Baby's first toys, of course. The mobile, blocks, string of hearts, and frame are perfect for those first few months, when baby's eyesight is developing. For safety reasons, make sure to remove the string of hearts and the mobile from the crib by the time baby can sit up on his or her own. As with all toys and items intended for baby, make sure all pieces are stitched together securely and check them periodically for loose parts.

Alphabet Blocks

MATERIALS

9 yds (8.2m) of ⅜-inch (1cm)-wide satin ribbon in black dot pattern

4 yds (3.6m) of ⅜-inch (1cm)-wide grosgrain ribbon in red

1 yard (1m) of ⅝-inch (1.5cm)-inch-wide ribbon in red and white check

1½ yds (1.5m) of ⅞-inch (2cm)-wide ribbon in red and white check

1 pkg premade Zach and Zoie ribbon zebras

⅝ yd (58cm) of muslin fabric

⅝ yd (58cm) of black and white gingham fabric

1 yd (1m) of white fabric

12 x 18-inch (30 x 50cm) piece of 3-inch (7.5cm)-thick foam rubber

Three ⅝-inch (1.5cm) white buttons

Fusible web

Electric knife

Tacky glue

DIRECTIONS

Note: Use ¼-inch (6mm) seams unless otherwise noted.

1. Use the electric knife to cut foam into six 3 x 6-inch (7.5 x 15cm) blocks. Glue two squares together with tacky glue to form three foam blocks, each one 6 inches (15cm) square. Allow glue to dry thoroughly.

2. For each block lining, cut six 6-inch (15cm) squares of muslin. Machine stitch squares together. Leave three sides of the last block open so that foam block can be inserted into lining. Place block in lining and stitch the opening closed.

3. For each block, cut six 6-inch (15cm) squares of gingham. Apply fusible web to back of white fabric. For each block, cut six 4-inch (10cm) squares of white fabric. Following manufacturer's instructions, fuse a white fabric square to the center of each gingham square. Cut lengths of ⅜-inch black dot ribbon and stitch ribbon around the edge of each white square.

4. Each block is made of six squares: three letters or numbers, one zebra, one bow, and one flower. TO MAKE THE NUMBERS AND ALPHABET LETTERS, see the illustration on pages 130–131. Note that letters A, B, and C are used on one block X, Y, and Z are used on another block, and the numbers 1, 2, and 3 are used on the third. The letters and numbers are made by cutting lengths of ⅜-inch red grosgrain ribbon and stitching them to the center of each white square. The dashed lines in the illustration indicate where ribbons are overlapped.

For each zebra square, stitch a ribbon zebra to the center of a white square. Following General Bow Techniques on page 140, make a small two-loop bow using the 3/8-inch (1cm) grosgrain ribbon and stitch to neck of zebra.

For each ribbon bow square, follow General Bow Techniques to make a two-loop bow with 1/3 yd (30.5cm) of 5/8-inch red and white checked ribbon and sew to center of white square.

For each flower square, cut four 6-inch (15cm) lengths of 3/8-inch red grosgrain ribbon. Form each length into a loop, overlap ends at center, and sew through center to form two petals. Continue to add loops to create an eight-loop flower shape. Sew button to center of flower and sew completed flower to center of white square.

5. For each block, stitch three letters or numbers, one zebra, one bow, and one flower square together. Leave three sides of last square unstitched so covered foam block can be inserted. Insert block and stitch opening closed.

"String of Hearts" Crib Decoration

MATERIALS

3⅓ yds (3.2m) of ⅜-inch (1cm)-wide grosgrain ribbon in red

3 yds (3m) of ⅝-inch (1.5cm)-wide novelty ribbon in black and white

2 premade Zippy ribbon zebras

Four ⅝-inch (1.5cm) white buttons

One 13-inch (33cm) square black gingham fabric remnant

6 x 13-inch (15 x 33cm) red gingham fabric remnant

Polyester fiberfill (one small package)

DIRECTIONS

1. Trace pattern onto gingham fabric. Cut two red and four black gingham hearts.

2. Sew ribbon zebras at center, on front and back of red heart. Cut two ⅜-yard lengths of ⅜-inch red grosgrain ribbon. Following General Bow Techniques on page 140, make each into a small two-loop bow and sew to neck of each zebra.

3. Cut four 24-inch (61cm) lengths of ⅜-inch red grosgrain ribbon. Following General Flower Techniques on page 139, make four ribbon flowers and stitch to front and back of each black heart.

Stitch Hearts Here

Stitch Hearts Here

Enlarge pattern by 20 percent

4. Machine-sew hearts together to make one red heart and two black hearts. Leave a small opening for turning. Stuff lightly with fiberfill and sew opening closed.

5. Placing red heart between black hearts, slipstitch sides of hearts together as indicated on pattern. Cut 5/8-inch novelty ribbon in half. Fold each length in half and slipstitch to the sides of the black hearts so that the toy can be tied onto the crib.

Ribbon Mobile

Note: Hang mobile out of baby's reach and remove it from the crib when he or she is able to sit up.

MATERIALS

8½ yds (7.75m) of 1½-inch (4cm)-wide gingham ribbon in black and white

6½ yds (6m) of 7/8-inch (2cm)-wide gingham ribbon in black and white

5 yds (4.5m) of 5/8-inch (1.5cm) wide polka-dot ribbon in red and white

4 yds (4m) of 3/8-inch (1cm)-wide grosgrain ribbon in red

3 5/8 yds (3.25m) of 5/8-inch (1.5cm)-wide gingham ribbon in red and white

2½ yds (2.5m) of 1½-inch (4cm)-wide polka-dot ribbon in black and white

2½ yds (2.5m) of 1½-inch (4cm)-wide polka-dot ribbon in white and black

4 premade Zippy ribbon zebras

1 each 14-inch (35.5cm), 10-inch (25.5cm), and 3-inch (7.5cm) Styrofoam wreaths

Hot glue gun and glue sticks

30-gauge white covered wire

DIRECTIONS

1. Wrap 14-inch wreath with 6½ yds (6m) of 1½-inch black and white gingham ribbon. Glue ends. Wrap 10-inch wreath with 6½ yds (6m) of 7/8-inch black and white gingham ribbon. Glue ends.

2. Measure the top of each wreath and insert eight pins into each to use as a guide for attaching ribbon as hangers. Make sure the pins are evenly spaced around the wreaths.

3. Cut four 20-inch (51cm) lengths of 5/8-inch red polka-dot ribbon. Cut four 20-inch lengths of 5/8-inch red and white check ribbon. Alternating ribbons, glue lengths securely to the 10-inch wreath at the points marked with pins. Note that ribbons should be glued to the wreath so that they pass over top of wreath and hang down to be attached to larger wreath.

4. Wrap 3-inch wreath with 2½ yds (2.5m) of 3/8-inch red grosgrain ribbon. Glue ends. Cut a 1-yard (1m) length of red polka-dot ribbon and run through wrapped wreath. Glue ends of dot ribbon to top inside of 10-inch wreath. Ribbon ends should be glued across from each other so that the wreath will hang evenly.

5. Pin ribbons hanging down from 10-inch wreath to 14-inch wreath. Ribbons should be pinned at the points marked. Make sure the wreaths hang evenly. Adjust ribbons and glue to larger wreath.

6. For zebra streamers, cut four 15-inch (38cm) lengths of red polka-dot ribbon. Stitch a ribbon zebra onto one end of each length. Cut remaining 3/8-inch red grosgrain ribbon into four equal lengths. Tie each length into small two-loop bow. Stitch bow to the neck of each zebra. Glue streamers to large wreath, matching up with each red polka-dot ribbon hanger.

7. For bow streamers, cut four 12-inch (30cm) lengths of red and white check ribbon. Cut remaining black and white gingham ribbon into four equal lengths. Form each gingham ribbon into a two-loop bow and wire at the center. Wrap one end of each check ribbon around the center of each bow. Glue streamers to wreath, matching up with each red and white check ribbon hanger.

8. Make two-loop bow from 1½-inch-wide polka-dot ribbons and glue to top of streamers on 14-inch wreath.

Zebra Frame

MATERIALS

$5/8$ yd (58cm) of $5/8$-inch (1.5cm)-
wide ribbon in red and white
check

$1/2$ yd (50cm) of $3/8$-inch (1cm)-
wide ribbon in black and white
check

1 pkg premade Zoie and Zack
ribbon zebras

5 x 7-inch (13 x 17.5cm) frame
with black edge

DIRECTIONS

1. Cut lengths of red and white check ribbon to fit around frame, next to black
edge. Miter corners and glue in place.

2. Glue premade ribbon zebras to upper left and lower right corners of frame.

3. Cut black and white ribbon in half and tie each into a small bow. Glue bows
to each zebra.

TAKING BETTER BABY PICTURES

✶ First, get your baby in a good mood. Your pictures will be most successful if the baby has been recently fed and changed, and is not tired or cranky.

✶ Focus on the baby, and make sure that he or she fills most of the frame. If you are too far away or are not clearly focused on your child, it will be harder to identify the subject of the picture.

✶ Eliminate distracting extras from the picture—your baby should be the undeniable star of the photo. A wide frame that includes lots of other people, furniture, toys, and other items draws attention away from your adorable little one!

✶ Reduce red-eye by taking your pictures outdoors or in a well-lit room. Because the flash is what causes the red-eye phenomenon, try shooting indoor pictures without it. Some doctors believe that the flash is bad for the eyes of young babies, so avoid it if you can and never use it for closeups. If all else fails and your baby ends up with glowing eyes in your pictures, your local photo shop may be able to take out the red-eye, or try a red-eye touch-up pen, which allows you to simply color in the red areas.

✶ Keep your camera handy so you can record all the spontaneous discoveries your baby makes and the delightful moments that occur each and every day. Too often, we reserve photo opportunities for "special" days such as birthdays, Christmas, or other celebrations. The quiet moments and daily routines can be every bit as special, and often make for the best pictures because everybody is relaxed and comfortable.

APPENDIX
THE ABCs OF RIBBON TECHNIQUE

THIS APPENDIX SERVES AS A general introduction to ribbon techniques and is a good review for those of you already familiar with ribbonwork. Before you begin your project, please look over the information here to help you choose the right ribbons for the projects in this book. Unless otherwise noted, the ribbons used are woven-edge ribbons, which means they are woven on looms, giving them finished selvedges. This is important because these ribbons may be both machine-washed and dry-cleaned, and are perfect for stitch-down application. If you are making a project that will not be washed or dry-cleaned, such as the picture frames, gift basket, or wastebaskets, craft or floral type ribbons may be used.

Each project's instructions include a materials list as well as references to the general techniques found in this section. Before you begin, make sure to have your basic supplies on hand. These include:

- Scissors • Sewing needles and thread • Glue gun and glue sticks
- Floral wire • Ruler • Tape measure • Pencil • Tacky glue •
Spray adhesive • Safety pins • Fabric glue • Sewing machine

General Flower Techniques

Ruffled Leaves

Cut ribbons to lengths specified. Cut one end of each ribbon into a sharp "V." Fold back the other end from raw edge. Beginning at folded end, machine-stitch with long gathering stitches down center of ribbon. Pull stitches slightly to gather. Pin in place and machine-stitch, stitching on top of gathering stitches.

Folded Leaves

Cut ribbons to 4 inches (10cm) long. Cut ribbon ends on the diagonal. Fold slightly off center. Hand-stitch in place.

Gathered Ribbon Rose

Cut wire-edged ribbon to desired length. Knot one end, and pull knot firmly toward end to secure. From opposite side, gently pull one wire, slowly gathering until entire side is completely ruffled and curling naturally. Wrap gathered ribbon around knotted end, forming a bud. Continue wrapping lightly so ribbon flares out and acquires an open rose effect. Tie wires together and trim. Adjust shape by fluffing or crumpling.

Ribbon Flower

Form each ribbon length into a loop, overlap ends, and sew through center to form two petals. Continue to add loops to create an eight-loop flower shape. Sew button to center of flower.

GENERAL BOW TECHNIQUES

To fasten a bow with wire, fold an 18-inch (50cm) length of wire in half. Place the folded wire underneath the chosen ribbon and wrap the wire around the center, inserting the wire ends through the loop to tighten. Pull the wire ends to secure, bringing one end around center again at back. To tighten, twist the bow—*not* the wire—a few times.

Two-Loop Bow and Variations

For a two-loop bow, cut a length of ribbon as specified in the project instructions. Wrap the ribbon back and forth, forming two loops with tails. Glue a small strip of ribbon around the ribbon loops to hold it in place. Ease the ribbon tail to the back of the bow.

For four-, six-, eight-, ten-, and twelve-loop bows, simply increase the number of loops before securing the center strip.

GENERAL SEWING TECHNIQUES

Applique Work

Following manufacturer's directions, fuse all applique fabrics to fusible web. Trace applique pattern pieces onto appropriate fabrics and cut them out. Fuse pieces in place on background panel. Using the satin stitch setting on your sewing machine, stitch over all raw edges of the fused shapes in the appliqued panel.

Buttonhole Stitch

This stitch is worked from left to right. Bring needle through fabric at A, holding the thread down with thumb; bring needle into fabric at B (about $1/8$ to $1/4$ inch away from edge of fabric). Bring needle back through at C, catching thread underneath needle tip, and pull gently.

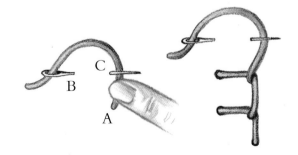

General Strip Piecing Techniques

Woven-edge ribbons are excellent for strip piecing work. They have two finished edges and are easily applied by hand, machine, or fusing, providing depth and texture. By following a few simple steps, you can make beautiful creations.

- Always work in same direction on both edges to prevent puckering.
- Ribbon is best applied to flat fabric before the garment is made up.
- Butt edges of ribbons carefully when stitching to create a smooth, even finish.

Strip piecing can be done in two methods for two different looks. The first method involves stitching the ribbon to lightweight fabric to give a firm, stable surface. The second method is to zigzag or featherstitch over the edges of both ribbons at the same time.

To Strip Piece: Cut ribbons in lengths as directed in individual project. Set zigzag or featherstitch to a narrow width and a length long enough to catch both ribbon edges. Hold two ribbon lengths with edges butted, and zigzag or featherstitch entire length of ribbons. Continue adding ribbons to outer edges in correct order until the required size is obtained. Treat joined and sewn ribbons as fabric and continue with individual project.

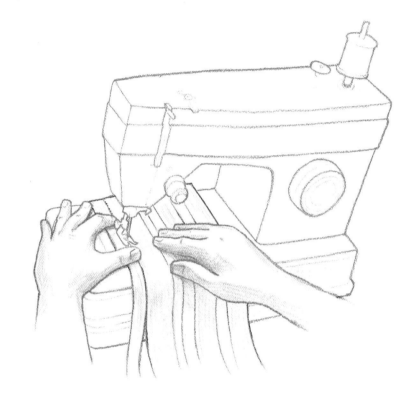

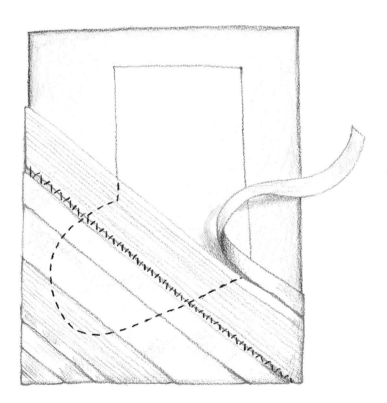

To Strip Piece on Fabric: Cut ribbons in lengths as directed in individual project. Mark a design line on fabric with disappearing marker, drawing toward center of project. Lay ribbon along the line and hold in place with a fabric glue stick or basting stitch. Straight-stitch along both edges. Continue working from center to edges. Trace pattern to be cut on ribbon-trimmed fabric and stitch on traced line. Cut just outside of traced line. Continue with individual project.

FURTHER READING

Bundles of Joy: A Book for New Moms. Andrews McMeel Publishing, 1998.

Fontanel, Beatrice, and Claire d'Harcourt. *Babies: History, Art, and Folklore.* New York: Harry N. Abrams, Inc., 1997.

Kalman, Bobbie. *Historic Communities: Games from Long Ago.* Crabtree Publishing Company, 1995.

Kalman, Bobbie, and David Schimpky. *Historic Communities: Old Time Toys.* Crabtree Publishing Company, 1995.

The Little Baby Book. Andrews McMeel Publishing, 1992.

Scurry, Pamela. *Cradle and All.* New York: Clarkson Potter, 1992.

Stoddard, Alexandra. *A Child's Place.* New York: Doubleday & Company, Inc., 1977.

Tuleja, Tad. *Curious Customs.* New York: The Stonesong Press, Inc., 1987.

Warner, Diane. *Complete Book of Baby Showers.* The Career Press, 1998.

INTERNET SITES FOR PARENTS

www.Kbkids.com
Resource for toys, product information, articles, questions and answers

www.BabyCenter.com
Resource for articles, safety, baby shower ideas, names, and much more

www.babystyle.com
Resource for baby products, maternity store, gift registry, and information

RESOURCES

Concord Fabrics Inc.
1359 Broadway
New York, NY 10018
(212) 760-0300
fabrics

Dan River Inc.
111 West 40th St.
New York, NY 10018
(212) 554-5613
fabrics

Daisy Kingdom
134 NW 8th
Portland, OR 97209
(503) 222-9033
chenille fabric

Fairfield Processing Corp.
88 Rose Hill Ave.
Danbury, CT 06810
(800) 243-0989
Poly-fil®, Soft Touch Pillow® inserts,
Hi-loft® quilt batting

FloraCraft
1 Longfellow Place
Ludington, MI 49431
(800) 253-0409
styrofoam wreaths

Hampton Art Stamps
19 Industrial Blvd.
Medford, NY 11763
(516) 924-1335
rubber stamps, art supplies

Hero Arts
1343 Powell St.
Emeryville, CA 94608
(800) 822-4376
rubber stamps and supplies

Peking Handicraft Inc.
1388 San Mateo Ave.
So. San Francisco, CA 94080
(650) 871-3788
lace handkerchiefs and doilies

Personal Stamp Exchange
360 Sutton Pl.
Santa Rosa, CA 95407
(707) 588-8058
rubber stamps and supplies

Simplicity Pattern Company
2 Park Avenue
New York, NY 10016
(888) 588-2700
commercial sewing patterns

Stampendous Inc.
1240 N. Red Gum
Anaheim, CA 92806
(714) 688-0288
rubber stamps and supplies

INDEX